Imagine Your Library's Future

CHANDOS
INFORMATION PROFESSIONAL SERIES

Series Editor: Ruth Rikowski
(email: Rikowskigr@aol.com)

Chandos' new series of books are aimed at the busy information professional. They have been specially commissioned to provide the reader with an authoritative view of current thinking. They are designed to provide easy-to-read and (most importantly) practical coverage of topics that are of interest to librarians and other information professionals. If you would like a full listing of current and forthcoming titles, please visit our web site www.chandospublishing.com or email info@chandospublishing.com or telephone +44 (0) 1223 499140.

New authors: we are always pleased to receive ideas for new titles; if you would like to write a book for Chandos, please contact Dr Glyn Jones on email gjones@chandospublishing.com or telephone number +44 (0) 1993 848726.

Bulk orders: some organisations buy a number of copies of our books. If you are interested in doing this, we would be pleased to discuss a discount. Please email info@chandospublishing.com or telephone +44 (0) 1223 499140.

Imagine Your Library's Future

Scenario planning for libraries and information organisations

STEVE O'CONNOR

AND

PETER SIDORKO

CP

CHANDOS
PUBLISHING

Oxford Cambridge New Delhi

Chandos Publishing
TBAC Business Centre
Avenue 4
Station Lane
Witney
Oxford OX28 4BN
UK
Tel: +44 (0) 1993 848726
Email: info@chandospublishing.com
www.chandospublishing.com

Chandos Publishing is an imprint of Woodhead Publishing Limited

Woodhead Publishing Limited
80 High Street
Sawston
Cambridge CB22 3HJ
UK
Tel: +44 (0) 1223 499140
Fax: +44 (0) 1223 832819
www.woodheadpublishing.com

First published in 2010

ISBN:
978 1 84334 600 5

© S. O'Connor and P. Sidorko, 2010

British Library Cataloguing-in-Publication Data.
A catalogue record for this book is available from the British Library.

Typeset by RefineCatch Limited, Bungay, Suffolk
Printed in the UK and USA.

Printed in the UK by 4edge Limited - www.4edge.co.uk

To Julia,
who is inspiring, challenging and encouraging.
In so many ways, you created this book.
Steve

For Nicole, Hannah and Maya.
For helping me imagine.
Peter

Contents

Preface

The environment in which libraries exist is made more difficult by three driving factors: firstly, the pervasive nature of the web; secondly, the financial pressures on libraries and their funding institutions; and thirdly, the perception that libraries no longer play a dominant role in the future of their institutions or communities. Indeed, the view is often held that libraries are 'leftovers' from bygone eras.

These factors are creating entirely new operating conditions for libraries. Library planners need fresh tools to revitalise their understanding of this new 'set of conditions'. Scenario planning, as a planning tool, has an impressive track record for organisational future-setting. Scenario planning does not provide the 'answer' but rather a series of viable options. This technique successfully offers fresh perspectives on organisational futures. In the library environment it is equally appropriate for different library sectors as well as for small and large consortium organisations.

Scenario planning is a tool used as a precursor to strategic planning. There is a clear distinction between strategic planning and scenario planning. Scenario planning is an imaginative process, creating stories of the different futures from which each organisation, their users and staff may choose. It is a series of tools to engage stakeholders, users and staff in the creation of new vital futures for the library or information agency. Strategic planning, on the other hand, is an administrative tool, often formulaic, allocating resources with which to meet the chosen future.

Without augmentation, the Strategic Planning tool does not visualise new futures for the library or information agency. Strategic Planning without prior Scenario Planning most often perpetuates the past; it allocates resources to projects and directions but does not have the capability to let go of former practices. Unaided, Strategic Planning was the dominant Planning tool of the 1960s and 1970s. Not now! Those older style Strategic Planners are retiring and the new generation of library managers – facing a future of ever accelerating change – need Scenario Planning to help their thinking.

The book

The book is a thought-provoking development of thinking on the future of libraries. It provides tools to assist all library and information professionals to re-conceptualise their future and that of their organisations. It challenges the foundations of many an understanding of what libraries could be. Infused into the text is the means by which the reader can benefit from the processes of Scenario Planning. The tools to draw insight and inspiration are those used in Scenario Planning. The chapters in this volume are new Scenarios for libraries. They are partly derived from successful Scenario Planning exercises actually completed over recent years. The readers of this book will gain new perspectives through developing different scenarios of library futures, as well as a clear understanding of how to replicate them in their own environment.

The book is presented in the following manner:

What are scenarios?

The first chapter will draw the readers immediately to the potential of new approaches when thinking about the futures of their libraries. It will briefly highlight what Scenarios are and how they can impact so strongly on the well-being and vitality of an organisation, its stakeholders and staff. It will discuss the merits of having different options to allow new and imaginative approaches to library futures.

The complexities of our informational environment

Looking at our current operating environment will be tempered here by creating perspectives of what has happened to our operations and what could happen. Before we can create Scenarios we need to understand what is happening in our immediate and wider environments. Attempts are made here to highlight the 'left-field' influences as we often do not see them until they are right upon us. Various tools and techniques will be used to illustrate these points and to use a backward-looking view to actually look forward. This will help the readers to understand the nature and power of Scenarios as stories of what has been and what could be.

The future and the past: models are changing

This chapter will look at where libraries and consortia have come from and the characteristics of their development, drawing on global examples as much as possible. The concept of the future will come into sharper relief as it is difficult to understand, let alone predict. This chapter will also deal with what has happened, what is happening and what will happen. It will especially deal with how we might begin to re-focus our thinking so that we can more easily and readily see the trends affecting us and our organisations. It will begin to reflect on how our library business models are changing.

Consortia are a relatively recent phenomenon emerging to meet needs of individual libraries to gain more traction on price and other negotiating issues. Consortia are now themselves merging and seeking new perspectives to assist their member libraries. There will be a discussion on how to begin the hard decisions to break out of the established mould; how to show leadership in achieving this. Strategies will be discussed as to how to assist in convincing others of the merits of a new approach and how to design relevant processes.

Understanding choices

When dealing with choices and ambiguity it is easy to become confined. This chapter will discuss this issue in the context of how to establish and execute the Scenario Planning process. There will be exercises designed to create a frame of mind in which we know that 'we can choose'. The Scenario Planning process is described in terms of how it operates, what the variable components are, what the critical success factors are and how to optimise application of the process. Implications of seemingly simple decisions are explored, as are the consequences of not looking forward and acting accordingly.

Toward a new way of thinking

The purpose of this chapter is to move ourselves and our staffs into a space where good ideas are not dismissed because they are too expensive, too staff intensive, too this or that. 'We cannot do this because of this or that or that or this!' It is a matter of moving people out of that mental space. This requires some effort and some skill. The skills and appropriate outlook will be explored in this chapter.

Designing your process

Scenarios can be best understood in everyday work and life situations. This chapter develops techniques to enable this to happen. This will grow the understanding of the Scenario approach at the institutional level.

Scenarios and implementation

This chapter is very practical, exploring techniques to get different forces in the institution to agree. to work together and to enable 'buy-in' to the process and the outcomes. This describes various approaches available to move toward the actual scenario construction. This approach will note that most processes will develop multiple Scenarios reflecting the range of choices which libraries have. How to deal with multiple scenarios will be crucial.

Choice, chance and (less than) certainty

It will be important to take stock as the Scenario creation process draws to a close and prepares for implementation. This chapter looks at the creation of an alignment between the Strategic Planning process and the operations plans. Identifying immediate/short-term/longer-term actions will be discussed from political and operational viewpoints.

Case studies

This technique has been used on a number of occasions and a number of actual scenarios are replicated in this chapter. These are some of the scenarios which have derived benefit from the very exercises and processes that are explored in earlier chapters.

Implementation and the impact of change (by Peter Sidorko)

Despite recent turbulence in the information world, successful change remains a difficult matter for implementation in libraries, and indeed for most organizations. As a major strategy for change in an organization, the Scenario Planning process must be introduced into the organisation by adopting many of the established success factors for change. Included among these are the identification of a problem (the reasons for change), the developing of a shared vision, communication and ultimately embedding the change. Despite such well established strategies in the literature, formulaic implementation is impossible.

Acknowledgments

This book has been a long time in gestation and is dedicated to all the librarians I have been privileged to work with and learn from in my career. Professor David Jones, as the Chair of CAVAL Collaborative Solutions, taught me much more than I could ever re-pay. Sue Henczel has always been a furnace of good ideas, practice and 'can do' approaches. I especially thank my staff at The Hong Kong Polytechnic University Library for their belief in and action toward what we imagined for our library's future.

David Hobbs provided many contributions as well as a thoughtful edit for the manuscript as it drew close to the end. I am always very grateful to John Jessup for his ideas and long friendship.

I want to thank my co-author Peter for his support, ideas and encouragement. Debbie Yuen has been wonderfully patient and helpful with manuscript corrections. I thank Rosa She for all her support and organisation.

This book is finally committed to my sons Damien, Dominic, Brendan and Richard whose future I thought I understood but whose chosen paths are far more interesting than my imagined ones.

Thank you one and all.

Steve O'Connor

List of figures, table and case studies

Figures

Table

Case Studies

About the authors

Steve O'Connor has extensive experience in managing large and small organisations, both income- and expenditure-based. His work demonstrates a research and futures focus, which has been developed to ensure library and information services achieve creative, relevant, efficient and cost-beneficial outcomes for all stakeholders.

Steve has researched, published, spoken, consulted and taught extensively in the areas of change, organisational management, information delivery, collection transition, scenario and strategic planning, and the wider library and information environment. He enjoys foundational and critical ongoing involvement in the development and implementation of digital information services, and in the provision of consortia strategies for compliance, service and financial improvement. He has held positions as the University Librarian in Australia and now in Hong Kong. He has been the CEO of a large consortium as well.

Currently, Steve is focused on the creation of new and sustainable business models for the future of libraries. He is also the Editor of the international, peer-reviewed journal, *Library Management* as well as *Library Management China*, which is building bridges to the Chinese Library communities.

Steve's significant work has earned him respect and an international recognition.

Peter Sidorko is the Deputy University Librarian at the University of Hong Kong, a position he has held since 2001. In this role Peter has day-to-day management responsibility for the full range of public services, technical services and technological developments for the entire University Library system, which consists of one main library and six branch libraries, a staff of approximately 240 and a collection in excess of 2.7 million physical volumes plus a vast digital collection. In his position he has been instrumental in initiating and directing change within the libraries.

As a part-time lecturer in the University of Hong Kong's Information Science programmes conducted through the Faculty of Education as well as through the University's continuing education school, he has recently taught subjects that have included: Change and Professional Development, The Information Society, Information Policy, Library Supervision and Management, Contemporary Library Management and Management of Information Agencies. He is a strong advocate of effective leadership and change in academic and research libraries.

The authors may be contacted via the publishers.

What are scenarios?

Have you ever stopped to consider how your library would function without:

- published content in digital form
- personal computers (as opposed to mainframes with terminals)
- the Internet

It is very difficult to imagine our present world without these three fundamental realities and yet only ten years ago, such things were just emerging. Imagine what the future might offer us ... ten years from now.

This book will offer you the tools with which to imagine that future or new futures.

When we talk of our individual plans for a holiday or a career, we are constructing future stories. Stories are the precursor to action. They help us to describe what might be. Imagine that you were able to re-invent your library's future. What would you do? Would you know what to change? Would you be able to convince your stakeholders and your colleagues about your proposed changes? Would you be confident to select just the right changes?

It is important to recognise that we develop a lot of stories before settling on an actual action plan. And so it is with scenarios. We should be developing a number of stories about the future of libraries. There are many possible stories about our organisations. Many cultures have passed their stories through their oral culture. In a similar way, other cultures have recorded their story on stone, papyrus or paper. These are historical stories. We will in this book be developing imaginative stories about our future – not our present or past. We just do not recognise that these stories exist or that these stories can be quite different from the present style of operation.

Stories are vastly underestimated as a tool for understanding the power of cultures and possibilities. Oral cultures use stories with great skill to perpetuate, even reinvigorate, what it means to belong to that particular culture. The stories sustain everything that it means to belong to and understand the culture and its history. Just as each family has stories of its past, its members and all their aspirations, so do our libraries. Libraries have stories about how they have done well and the impact which they have had. Living in the library culture as we do, we often tend to believe without necessarily questioning the nature and veracity of those stories. We have heard that libraries are 'at the heart of our organisations or communities'; we have heard that libraries are the only organisations that can deliver information; we have heard or learnt that publishing is the only way in which information can be presented as literature or factual information. These are stories which we accept, often without questioning. This book is committed to cultivating *new* stories about libraries and librarians.

Scenarios, which are stories that are constructed with informed views and knowledge, will be developed by the readers of this book using described techniques and approaches. These scenarios will be stories of possibilities; not rejecting the past, but clearly allowing and cultivating new possibilities. Scenario Planning is what we need to be engaged in prior to this action. We need to allow for the fact that we have choices which can be articulated through stories, and where each of these stories can be considered as potential futures, before deciding on the future direction of our libraries. But in all of this we need to use our imagination, informed by knowledge of our profession, the industry we work in and the future, or futures, that beckon us.

The future is not linear

> We were making the future, he said, and hardly any of us troubled to think what future we were making. And here it is! (H.G. Wells)

The future is often seen on a continuum with the present, in a linear relationship, as a simple extension of the present. We often expect that what we do today will be different to what we do tomorrow; but not so radically different. In this articulation of the future we are powerless to affect it. We believe that it will just happen. A linear view of the past, through the present then into the future is not a forward-looking continuum but rather a backward-looking expression. This is achieved by looking from the future and imagining that our path to this position has been entirely linear. The linearity is an imposition on history to explain events, to set them in a context and to present it as being the best way to reach that point in time. It is useful to note the concept of linearity as we will then remember that the history we lived through is riddled with decision points; points or times when decisions are made which will directly affect that future. If we remember those collective decision points we will easily see that the path to the future is not straight or linear.

3

It is difficult to imagine how we can improve on our present ways of doing things. We can visit an art gallery and view many forms of artistic expression and think silently to ourselves: 'Well, that is interesting. I cannot imagine any better ways to express feelings, emotions and views of the world than what I have seen today in this gallery collection.' The range of human emotion, imagination and perspectives on our world is incredible. As each age throws up new interpretations and insights into the human condition, these insights can often contain the germs of new approaches, of different ways in which to respond to challenges confronting a society, an organisation or even a culture. As an aside, it is widely recognised that sometimes the most insightful and different artistic expressions have come through psychotic episodes, or mental illness. Artists 'see' the world differently. They can represent the world through their imagination and enable us to begin to 'see' what they 'see'. Their art will often give the viewer an entirely different view of what is being represented.

> How ignorant of the future we are, and how emotional when it arrives and fails to conform to expectations. (Peter Bernstein[1])

We can see our favourite sporting individuals or teams perform at the heights of kinetic excellence, achieving feats of sporting prowess which we cannot imagine being bettered. Their training methods have led to world records; have led to feats of endurance which have been unsurpassed. It is almost impossible to predict how fast people can run, how fast they can swim, how much they can endure, or how a team can dominate its opposition in such a spectacular and generation-shattering manner. In these areas of kinetic intelligence we are confronted with excellence pushing the boundaries of what we thought was possible. In other words,

Figure 1.1 Futures are not linear

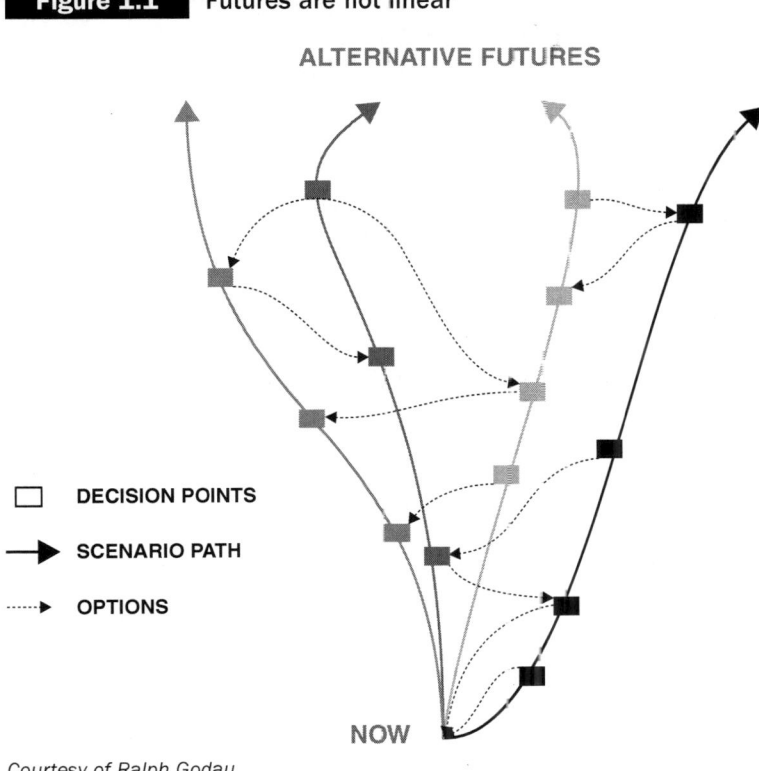

ALTERNATIVE FUTURES

DECISION POINTS

SCENARIO PATH

OPTIONS

NOW

Courtesy of Ralph Godau

we are forced to accept that what we thought was not possible is now not only possible but is a reality.

What is the value of scenarios?

- Scenario planning generally identifies a number of scenario paths leading to alternative futures.
- Each scenario has points in time when decisions must be made to continue or move onto another path (options) based on what is learnt and what has changed.

- Ability to move onto another path (number and type of options) depends on the path you are on and the type of internal and external factors influencing that move.

Exercise

We all have choices. It is important to remember that we are constantly choosing between one option and another. The choices we make sometimes have little impact, yet sometimes they can be momentous.

Part 1

1. Consider how you arrived at work today.
2. Consider the alternative ways you could go home after work.
3. Consider travel arrangements which have changed through no choice of our own.

Part 2

1. Explore the consequences of what might have happened if another choice had been made.
2. Consider those acquaintances who have missed a particular plane, train or bus trip with sometimes tragic consequences.
3. Have you made choices which might have had quite different consequences?

The future impacting on libraries

The Internet was only recently a concept in the mind of Tim Berners-Lee and is now a reality which has been earth-shattering in its impact. But what will its impact be beyond the present? The Internet came on the practical horizon in the early 1990s and we puzzled over this set of computer network connections that were almost like neural connections in our minds. The connections grew and grew and became more and more complex. In the early stages, we would never have had an appreciation of how the Internet would impact on the way we communicate and deliver services and information. We started to communicate with each other via e-mail and very quickly we have become dependent on this mode of communication. We then started to see applications which were previously local only but are now being beamed much more widely into the global audience. From a library perspective, this development facilitated the sharing of library catalogues, the data in them, the digitisation and sharing of library resources, the evolution of the e-journal article, the delivery of digital items direct from supplier to client without the intervention of the library staff at all and the Open Access movement.[2] The Internet clearly is having a profound effect on the world, the way in which we do business, the way in which we relate to each other and the way in which we deliver services and content. Joshua Meyrowitz famously used the phrase 'No sense of place' to describe the impact of electronic media on social behaviour. He might have also used the phrase to describe the impact of the Internet on libraries.[3] The Internet is sharply changing our organisational structures and services. Real estate agents now conduct far fewer home visits but have the house open across the Internet. Libraries are having their content much more available on the Internet and need new skills and staff to achieve this. Our organisations are being re-shaped, our staff re-skilled or new types of staff employed.

As libraries and information services are inextricably caught up in this maelstrom swirling around us, it is difficult to see the world outside the whirlpool as the changes seem to be constant. In fact, the only constant we have is change. If from a planning point of view change is a constant, it is so easy to see how our library and information service staffs find it wearing, find it frustrating, find it almost overwhelming at times. The reaction to change from staff can be a *passive aggressive* stance, which is understandable if they cannot be involved in the planning, even at the perimeter, and simply have change thrust upon them.

Another challenge of our modern lives is to deal with and relate to other aspects of technology. We have moved so quickly in our lifetimes from the hard disc vinyl records to the reel-to-reel tape, to the cassette tape, to the CD, to the DVD and now to the digital. The digital format and delivery have become dominant for all forms of contents. We have seen communication formats squeezed into these new vehicles for communication. Music was the first and the easiest; movies were more difficult but have now moved and are being delivered in the DVD format, which is itself undergoing changes in its technology. Journal content has moved from the print page quickly through the CD, the juke

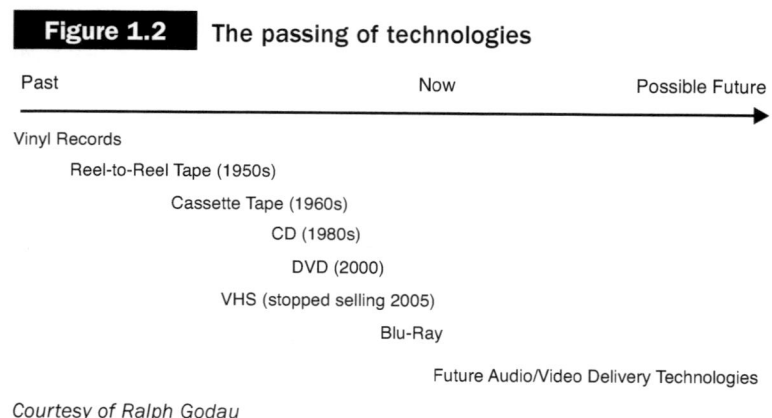

Figure 1.2 The passing of technologies

Past	Now	Possible Future

Vinyl Records

Reel-to-Reel Tape (1950s)

Cassette Tape (1960s)

CD (1980s)

DVD (2000)

VHS (stopped selling 2005)

Blu-Ray

Future Audio/Video Delivery Technologies

Courtesy of Ralph Godau

box and now into the virtual. The mainframe computer was quickly overtaken and superseded by the power and empowerment of the much preferred personal computer, where individuals were able to work in their own personal space and now via wireless to be creative, to be productive and to be less and less dependent on existing work structures. We have seen technological devices develop from the transistor radio, to the Walkman which used cassette tapes, to the iPod and now to the ubiquitous mobile phone. The impact of technology cannot be underestimated. The availability and appropriateness of a technology can, if allowed, change the essential ways in which we conduct our business. One example of this which is currently in vogue is to access the library's online catalogue from the mobile phone so that time spent in the library is minimised. Mobile devices for information access are still to reach this zenith of popularity.

Marshall McLuhan, the Canadian cultural and media guru from the 1960s, ascribed to electronic media the capacity to shape the culture and politics of our time. Different media would be embracing of change while others would be more remote. McLuhan saw that the power of each medium would impact on all who come to use that medium. So the Gutenberg printing press created the capacity for individual study in isolation and for ideas to be transmitted so much more easily. McLuhan believed that we should have a *rear vision mirror* view of history in our lives. He meant that we always see the present in terms of our past and he believed that because of this we are not able to deal with the future until it happens to us. Marshall McLuhan inspired many to look at the electronic media in our lives in a different way. He saw technology as a determinant of social arrangement and change. If McLuhan achieved anything it was to highlight the impact which communication media have on social communication and interaction. Libraries have always been impacted by technology over the centuries, especially now and certainly into the future.

We read widely that the role of the physical library is being directly influenced by the technology which libraries have embraced to deliver content to their users. This technological impact has led to the suggestion that libraries are largely irrelevant, even obsolete. These claims are often supported with the view that it is only necessary to organise the digital connections and all else is irrelevant. Yet we are seeing a revitalisation of libraries as social spaces where information and creativity interact. It is a renaissance. But where is this movement going? Is it a new strategic direction or purpose? What will be the impact of the next technological development on the physical library? What will be the impact of this new type of library space on the nature of the library service? Where will the vast legacy collections[4] be located and how will they be made available? Perhaps these changes are just happening without intentional purpose or direction.

Earlier in this chapter we began to look forward and found that there are limits to our imagination and that we think about the future as a linear extension of the present and the past. Often, the future is seen either as a series of crises or as the utopia. The Chinese language has a word called *Wei Ji* which means *crisis*. Literally this Chinese word has two components: *Wei* meaning *danger* and *Ji* meaning *opportunity*. For every future, *Wei Ji* is probably a very appropriate term or descriptor. Too often we are beguiled by the danger in a situation and confused by or blinded to the opportunity. Uncertainty of purpose and the lack of clear direction both contribute to this sense of crisis. The use of Scenario Planning as a set of tools enables us to begin to deal with the opportunity.

What is the future and does science fiction predict the future?

The concept of the future can be described on a continuum from the past through to the present. This, of course, is a simplistic if not overly simplistic description of a concept which has held writers and thinkers in awe for an eternity. There has long been a fascination with the future, in knowing what could be, what will be and, by inference, influencing the outcomes through foreknowledge. The concept that there is a linear relationship between the past and the future is also a misconception. It is popular to describe 'progress' as moving our society from one point to another along a pre-ordained path of development. Yet history does not move in straight lines; developments in our society are not linear either. The future is achieved through spates of discovery or innovation and unexpected paths of development. The future can also be regressive, and thus is very hard to predict.

The unpredictability of the future can be seen in such disasters as the Cambodian Pol Pot regime, where civilisation clearly regressed into a terrible form of savagery; the potent advances with stem cell research hold us spellbound as they threaten to solve so many genetic disorders and promise cures for previously unsolvable human conditions. Technology is often seen as the saviour of our society, leading it to bigger and better things. But often, the creation of new technologies leads to great sadness and despair. The advent of nuclear technologies simultaneously holds both great hope and despair. Great hope as a 'clean' environmental force delivering energy but despair in that there is no way of controlling the waste and in the hands of malevolent forces it could cause untold harm and misery. So 'progress' does not hold good or indeed bad values; in other words it is neither good nor evil. It is the use to which a development is put which dictates its moral perspective.

This discussion highlights that new technologies and new developments are not necessarily good or useful. They are not manichean! It is the uses to which they are put which will determine their value. Technology alone cannot be relied upon for good outcomes in our libraries.

Science fiction literature in the Western tradition has been rich and laced with imagination about the future. Writers such as H.G. Wells invented time machines to transport us physically into other worlds, while also creating adventures which were spectacular and enthralling and giving us a new way of looking at the future. In many ways Wells predicted some aspects of the future and stimulated our imagination for what could be. His classic book *War of the Worlds* built on existing knowledge of other worlds, yet created a whole new genre of possibilities and technologies. An article in the *New Scientist*[5] asked 'Whether science fiction is dying'. One commentator suggests that we are living the future of science fiction. 'The most useful thing I've learned from science fiction is that every present moment, always, is someone else's past and someone else's future.'[6] A crucial understanding in scenario creation and planning is that there are many views which usefully contribute to new understandings. There is no such thing as perfect knowledge. The economic concept of *asymmetric information*[7] describes the observation that some people know more about some things than other people. In many senses this is an unremarkable observation and yet there is a very significant literature surrounding this economic thought. To some extent it is possible to arrive at average views or moderate views by trying to accommodate everyone's views. In Scenario Planning we need to draw on as many views as possible but not to 'dumb them down'. It is important to keep as many views as possible on the table through the process. James Gunn's 'Libraries in Science Fiction'[8] relates how the concept of the library has, for the most part, been fictionalised as the human brain in various science fiction classics. He recounts how the human brain is seen as a 'library'; retrieving knowledge and information and making the connections. The significant books in this view include Robert Heinlein's *Universe* (1941), David H. Keller's *The Cerebral Library* (1931) and Jorge Luis Borges's *The Library of Babel* (1956). The conceptualisation of the library in science fiction literature, as we might know it, provides quite a different view of what a library is and what it means to have a library. Or does it? Perhaps this is one scenario of what could be.

Something to think about

The only way of discovering the limits of the possible is to venture a little way past them into the impossible (Arthur C. Clarke[9])

Change

Barack Obama is quoted as saying: 'You can't stop change from coming … you can only usher it in and work out the terms. If you're smart and a little lucky, you can make it your friend.'[10] We have much evidence of the amount of change which our current society is experiencing.

Marshall McLuhan once famously described his work as 'difficult stuff'. He was referring to his theorising about the impact of media on our lives and the ways in which it shapes our society. His adage, 'the medium is the message', became famous in the 1960s and 1970s. While he did not live to see the Internet begin to dominate our social and commercial communications, there is no doubt that he would have had strong and meaningful insights into the impact it would have.

An initial view of the Internet

The best place to start when considering the Internet is to realise how radically different it is as a medium. Marshall McLuhan was correct when he said: 'The medium is the message':

> The medium is not only the message. The medium is the mind. It shapes what we see and how we see it. The printed page, the dominant information medium of the past 500 years, molded our thinking through, to quote Neil Postman, 'its emphasis on logic, sequence, history, exposition, objectivity, detachment, and discipline.' The emphasis of the Internet, our new universal medium, is altogether different. It stresses immediacy, simultaneity, contingency, subjectivity, disposability, and, above all, speed.[11]

This is the most important aspect to remember about the Internet and our future libraries: the technologies we use shape the way we operate and how we relate to each other and our users.

As cited by John Markoff,[12] the number of publicly available Internet pages has risen in just ten years from 3.5 billion pages in 1999 up to over 30 billion pages in 2009. The number of hosts on the Internet in 2007 was 433 million. The number of private Internet pages is a multiple factor of this. The current mode of vanity publishing is the blog and, according to Technorati's *State of the Blogosphere 2009*,[13] more than 133 million blogs have been tracked by them since 2002. While the value of information available through the Internet is overwhelming, many of these pages reach the public area only through subscription. They include billions of pages of journal articles, e-books, and reference works available through powerful library services. The rates of growth of these indicators do not show any signs of slowing down. This phenomenon is often described as information glut or overload. But overload is fast becoming even more complex. An additional overlay to all of this is that China now has the greatest number of Internet users in the world, numbering 253 million with 84.6 per cent of them with broadband access. China has 39.5 per cent of the world's Internet users. The United States has 214 million persons online.[14] In late 2009, it was announced that domain names will in future be in a variety of languages. Thus will inevitably change the flavour of the Internet.

The success of the Internet can be measured in various ways. One is to recognise that there is an increasing problem for suitable Internet names to be found when they are all in English. Users are resorting to longer and longer names. In addition, bodies such as ICANN, which controls Internet protocols and domain names, are investigating new domain names such as .eco for ecological issues, .sport for sporting matters, etc. There is also strong interest in creating domain names for ethnic or cultural groups such as the Maoris from New Zealand or the Sami from Sweden. There could also be domain names for language groupings with Hindi, Putonghua or many other choices. This indicates that there is a sense that people see some form of identity through their domain names or Internet address. They also wish to be able to communicate within groupings as well as achieving the unexpected or that they 'feel lucky'. In a relatively short space of time, say mere years, the Internet has grown from being a novel communication network for defence researchers to an incredible web for seemingly anything and everything. If we find the present Internet environment difficult to comprehend and predict, it is worth applying the imagination to the plethora of opportunities and impacts which an Internet with the vastly increased variety of domain names would have. The wide range of scenarios, with such a differently structured Internet, would most assuredly have a dramatic effect on the library and its services.

The Library at Alexandria in the first century AD was able to boast that it had collected all the manuscripts known to be in existence at that time. Now, no such claim could be possible. The rate of information being thrust at us is such that it not only makes it difficult to find reliable authentic information but also almost impossible to determine and absorb the correct information. While new scenarios can be constructed to cope with the volume of information on the Internet, new ways need to be established to address the authenticity, reliability or even the accuracy of this information.

Scenarios, as will be demonstrated in this book, are a way of imagining and articulating new, future ways of dealing with difficult issues. Peter Schwartz is famous as the author of *The Art of the Long View* and a leading advocate of scenario planning:

> Scenarios are a tool for helping us to take a long view in a world of great uncertainty. The name comes from the theatrical term 'scenario' – the script for a film or play. Scenarios are stories about the way the world might turn out tomorrow, stories that can help us recognise and adapt to changing aspects of our present environment. They form a method for articulating the different pathways that might exist for you tomorrow,

and finding your appropriate movements down each of those possible paths. Scenario planning is about making choices *today* with an understanding of how they might turn out.[15]

Scenarios have been used by business and the military to explore options and unpredictable circumstances which might develop for their businesses or in geopolitical environments. They prove especially valuable in enabling people to think about issues and options which they do not ordinarily allow themselves to think about. These techniques are now also being increasingly used in the information world. These scenarios can operate at simple or complex levels. As with our own lives, there are choices to be made daily. We have choices in how we travel to work each day and how we return home. Choices that we make can have inconvenient, stark or even tragic consequences. We all recognise circumstances where our futures might have been different if we had chosen to walk one day, instead of riding a bicycle or had been two minutes later arriving at a particular place. It is far better to choose a future, rather than having it chosen for you.

When we apply this logic at levels of increasing complexity, change becomes ever more important if we are to position our information entities to be able to deliver high-quality responses to expressed information need. Constructing scenarios can be as complicated as a game of chess in which each player, on each move, has an increasingly large range of options and permutations to consider. Scenarios seek to harness such complexities in order to form manageable options.

In dealing with the information world there can be any number of future scenarios. A number of possible scenarios are explored over the coming pages. The scenario can challenge our conventional thinking about situations which we might accept unquestioningly. The scenario which suggests that we return to past traditional publishing models will not be entirely successful in an Internet age. Many people now have access to the web and may instantly become authors. The circulation figures of newspapers in western countries are declining.

Newspapers in a number of developing countries are thriving. This is especially the case in China and India. As such, the print vehicle is performing very well financially. In China, most of the publishing industry, as revealed in official statistics, is concentrated around Shanghai and the Yangtze River Delta. This is not the case with print newspapers which are very strong in the far west of China and Xinjiang.[16] Part of the reason for this is the large ethnic diversity of that province.

While newspapers in the United States are failing financially, they are also struggling to find a business model in the Internet environment. With this conflicting evidence different scenarios can emerge as to the possible futures for print and Internet-based newspapers.

The size of Internet populations has already been explored in earlier pages of this chapter. The largest Internet populations are now more in China and India than in the 'West'. The Internet users in China number more than the total population of the United States. This is changing the flavour, character and direction of the Internet. The ethnic character of the web is also changing, with large populations of different ethnic groupings realising the capacity of the Internet. Disturbances in Xinjiang with the Uyghur and with the political opposition in Iran were heavily influenced and powered by electronic media.

In constructing scenarios for the future of newspapers, we can see that they are sharply impacted upon by factors such as emerging Internet populations and different ethnic groupings with their aspirations. That there are changes to domain name regulations to allow for languages other than English merely extends the viability and power of these potential scenarios.

Copyright is in the public domain. Plagiarists are found relatively easily on the Internet, as evidenced in recent cases involving a politician in Australia as also with a number of other countries, through the use of software tools such as *Turnitin*. A Chinese software version can now also be used to detect plagiarism. In academic circles plagiarism matters but it is not perhaps so important to the future world of blogs, wikis and other alternative sources of news and opinion. It has been suggested, in places such as *The Economist*, that copyright may deter creativity. Traditionally – and certainly in academic publishing circles – it is critically important to acknowledge the words of other authors. It is an academic 'crime' not to do so. The argument is often made that culture affects attitude and practice toward copyright. The reverence for the teacher (*laucher*) is very strong in Chinese culture. It is argued that the quoting of that teacher is a sign of reverence. How could a student express an idea better than the teacher's words? So there are different attitudes and practices concerning copyright and the acknowledgement of attributed words in different parts of the world.

A scenario can emerge from this discussion that copyright as a legal concept could change, or could be applied in different ways in different cultures, in different circumstances. Copyright in the commercial would have a much stronger, harsher and punitive aspect to it. If an organisation holds copyright for a particular invention, product or artistic expression then they clearly wish to protect the revenues which may flow. Any loss of sales obviously impedes the economic viability of the organisation. As a result, working to extend the copyright protection of a product becomes very important to an organisation. The extension of the protection of copyright recently under law from 'Lifetime plus 50 years' to 'Lifetime plus 70 years' is often known as the 'Donald Duck clause'. This is because Walt Disney's Donald Duck character would have come out of copyright and thus been free for anyone to use if the copyright had not been extended. So expect more extension to the copyright protection clauses as Donald Duck gets older.

As discussed elsewhere, the Open Access movement aims to make materials much more available, and free if at all possible. The scenario which may emerge from these ideas concerns the justifiable length of copyright and the pressure to enable ideas to be freely available on the Internet. Various positions and possibilities can be determined in this area of copyright. As complex as it is, scenarios can and should be developed contrasting one position as opposed to another. These scenarios can then be run against other tensions such as the Internet, the growth of the Internet in different cultures, or the use of the Internet and copyright by different ethnic groupings.

Other scenarios may deal with the amount of education we need as to the sources of reliable information and/or which author blogs are professional and responsible. Dealing with the amount of information available on the Internet is formidable indeed. Dealing with the issue of accuracy or authenticity of the information available through those sites is another issue again. For example, a far right-wing organisation was recently found to have constructed a website to provide an alternative view on the life of Martin Luther King. The site was professional in appearance but totally misleading as to the information it contained. 'This is a website produced by a white power organisation and is one of the best/worst examples of a site that is trying to pass itself off as something entirely different. Proceed with caution on this one.'[17] The scenario being developed here relates to accuracy or inaccuracy of information. It may also relate to issues of censorship. The scenario can construct or apply to scenarios in any or all of the issues which we have discussed already in this chapter.

A tool to use in this act of scenario construction was made prominent by Clayton Christenson[18] in *The Innovator's Dilemma* that disruptive technologies fundamentally change our total technological interactions. According to this theory, a disruptive technology might be the PC, which totally replaced the mainframe and led to the ascendancy of the Microsoft Corporation and the power of the individual on the Internet; another might be the PDA (Personal Digital Assistant), which mostly replaced the paper diary; and now the mobile phone is absorbing the diary and a host of other functions to be a disruptive technology to the earlier two technologies. There will be more discussion of disruptive technologies and their impact in a later chapter. An extension of this thought is that disruptive innovations fundamentally change the rules by which marketplaces operate and are controlled. Evidence of this can be found in the United States Presidential election campaign by Barack Obama, which mustered unprecedented financial and moral support from individuals across the Internet. It has been noted widely in the press that the traditional fund-raising approach by Hillary Clinton in her political campaign among the power brokers and the 'big money end of town' worked but nonetheless failed to match the innovative approach of her opponent. Successfully predicting innovation or disruptive influences can enable organisations to achieve positions of future strength before the influence has firmly embedded its position.

A few possible scenarios have been offered here to explore possible futures caused by the impact of the Internet on communication, ideas, information and understanding. Other scenarios are clearly possible. The impact of thinking and preparing for changes with such possibilities lies in the basis of having sound and stimulating methodologies by which order can be created out of seeming chaos. It is also a way of recognising complexity and different, even divergent, paths to future positions.

That we talk of change as much as we do is a clear indication that many of us find it difficult to relate to or cope with change. Change can be unsettling. In the workplace, the less influence we have over what change occurs and how it occurs can lead to anxiety and resistance to change. Those who are less powerful in an organisation will inevitably suffer most in this regard. Lower-level staff have little control over their work flows and directions and can, in these circumstances, be very resistant to change which they did not foresee or that they do not understand or that they feel threatened by. President Obama in 2009 made a compelling and indeed convincing case for change in US society and its economy. In many senses this case was made so much easier because of the obvious and widespread observation by the US populace (and also the world, although they do not get the chance to vote in the United States) of the need to do something different.

This is not always the case for staff, clients and managers within library and information service environments as there is not always an obvious case for change. The need for change is perhaps more obvious with an aging workforce and where members of that workforce have been in their present roles for very long periods of time. When combining this reluctance to change with the increasing average age of staff, the task of re-shaping an organisation can be very difficult indeed. Engagement in the process of determining a new future is an ideal way to enable staff to participate in shaping the future direction of the organisation for which they work. The Scenario Planning process enables engagement, allows gradual understanding of the environment in which organisations find themselves, encourages choices between futures and enables shared ownership of the outcomes.

The Chief Executive of the popular MTV Networks, Judy McGrath, believes that 'change has to be in everyone's DNA, personally and professionally'.[19] It seems that we are being subjected to unprecedented amounts of change, the only constant in our lives. We all feel that the rate at which the change is taking place is constant and swift. We can only notice this rate of change with hindsight but we need to bear this prospect in mind as we look forward. A senior career in libraries today will have spanned the time where 5×3 catalogue cards were produced in a handwritten form, to where they were produced in multiple copies (for added entries and so on) by vendors, through to the MARC record for online catalogues and now the metadata processes. This is a spectacular amount of change in the space of less than three decades. And yet, despite McGrath's belief, change is not part of our DNA and the human spirit often longs for periods of stability.

It is important to recognise that there has been much change and also that it is beneficial to be able to measure that rate of change. In a narrower sense, each of us can see this rate of change through McLuhan's *rear vision mirror* view of our own history. We only have to look at events in our past and then to recollect how much change has occurred since that event. By looking back to a particular development, one can often readily witness how short a time period has elapsed since that development. By taking one's mind back to that time and remembering forward it can be seen how difficult it is to accurately predict or even understand the future from a point in one's past. For instance, by looking backward to when microfiche catalogues came into existence, one can remember how liberating they were. The microfiche catalogue, in many senses, was the first library catalogue produced using the power of the computer to manipulate and organise data. It enabled many sets of the catalogue to be produced so that they could be located on all floors of the library, could be located in academic departments elsewhere on campus, and could be exchanged with other libraries for quick identification of held resources. It was revolutionary. Remembering back to the time it made its appearance in libraries in the late 1970s to early 1980s, it was difficult to imagine the exact future which we have today a mere three decades on. It was, however, clear, at least in trend terms, that the computer was going to drive the change, the potential for further enhancements. The computer had already enabled the production of multiple card catalogue sets for each title and now had produced the microfiche catalogue. But what would the form of the future catalogue be?

Another instance to think about is to ask oneself when you became aware that the Internet would be a vehicle to transport library content? Already in the 1980s major subject indexes such as Index Medicus and actual journal content were being produced on CDs. The number of CDs that were required for the rapidly increasing range of content meant that it soon became apparent that a 'jukebox' was needed to efficiently manage the large numbers of discs. Soon there would be a need for many 'jukeboxes'. Then it became clear in the early 1990s that this journal content could be made available across the Internet. Now, a mere decade and a half later, the Internet has became so pervasive and perhaps intrusive to our lives. But remembering back to the first time when there was awareness of this potential is a moment of some excitement. Excitement in that this was indeed an even more radical development in the potential for the library to reach out beyond its walls and deliver content to where the user was physically located.

So the exercise of remembering back and then looking forward from that remembered time is a very useful exercise to help us understand rates of change. It also helps us understand that change will happen but that it is most likely to happen much sooner than we can project or predict. Change will wait for no person. This will be dealt with again later in the book.

Something to think about

'We know the future will outlast all of us, but I believe that all of us will live on in the future we make'. He concluded: 'I have lived a blessed time'. (Edward M. Kennedy[20])

Change of attitudes toward the future

In so far as it is possible, we need to shape our future, rather than letting the future happen to us. It is apparent that we have many possible futures open to us but the difficulty lies in identifying those futures and in choosing wisely amongst them. In more optimistic times people believe that resources inevitably follow to support growth. Today, there is a widespread pessimism, even fatalism, about the state of the world's environment which, couched with the severe economic downturn, is making people blind to positive opportunities. It is once again worthwhile remembering the Chinese word *Wei Ji* meaning danger and opportunity. They go 'hand-in-hand'. The scenario planning methodologies aim to assist and direct thinking in a constructive sense, even through emerging darker resource moods. In times of dark moods toward the future, the first thing that has to change is how we allow ourselves to think about the future. If we allow ourselves to begin to think about solutions, then the methodologies taught in this book will greatly open the possibilities and/or opportunities.

Development of scenarios as a discipline

For the future library to survive and prosper, the continuous alignment of its strategic direction with the demands of the environment is vital, especially when the speed of changes is rapid, and the scope extensive. However, changes that are unpredictable and complex in nature can sometimes be very threatening. In the face of uncertainty, psychological attachment to, and the defence of, what is destined to change can be dangerous. When library managers underestimate the impact of the emerging trends on their traditional roles and values, they are not positioning their library and themselves to capitalise on the changes emanating from these trends. On the other hand, if the threat of change is overestimated, yet one's abilities to shape the future are underestimated, one might still be locked into inaction in decision-making.[21] Coping patterns of 'bolstering failing strategy, procrastination and buck-passing' are identified as the typical signs of avoidance behaviours in responses to threatening change.[22] As noted by Pierre Wack, inertia and failure to decide is often rooted in 'the inability to see an emergent novel reality by being locked inside obsolete assumptions'.[23]

To free planners from obsolete assumptions, to overcome decision inertia and perceptual blind spots, a new planning tool called 'Scenario Planning' emerged in the 1960s. The US government initially applied it during the Cold War for geopolitical and military analysis. In the 1970s Royal Dutch Shell pioneered its use in the corporate sector and successfully prepared the company for the oil crisis in 1973.[24] Since then, scenario planning has been widely applied in both public and private sectors for product innovation, organisational re-engineering, public policy analysis, city planning, crime prevention, and NGO services.[25] Numerous articles in management journals have been published recording how creative decision makers embrace it as a tool to stimulate organisational learning,[26] to change organisation culture,[27] and to challenge deeply held beliefs.[28] A consultancy firm registered TAIDA (Tracking, Analysing, Imaging, Deciding, Acting) as its trademark and the name of the framework is now used in 'hundreds of scenario planning projects for public and private business and organisations'.[29] By systematically identifying and analysing the relationship between the critical driving forces in the external and internal environment, leveraging the different perspectives of a wide spectrum of stakeholders and experts, and imagining different possibilities and corresponding strategies, managers are better prepared for action as the future unfolds.

In the late 1990s, the American Library Association published a handbook providing tips on writing the scenario plots for public libraries[30] in utilising the scenario planning process. Information professionals in special libraries were also encouraged to apply scenario planning not only for internal library planning, but also to 'help their leaders understand that they provide insight to the organisation and that they don't just catalog and warehouse data'.[31] Steven J. Bell contended that the scenario approach could be applied to achieve a sustainable development of academic libraries.[32] In order to preserve its traditional core values, the library could take up new roles as a primary change agent. To achieve this, library managers are challenged to adopt scenario planning as a strategic and learning tool to visualise alternative futures that could be probable, possible, and, most importantly, a preferred future for them to construct. A matrix of scenarios, characterised as 'failing', 'conventional', 'technocentrist' and 'transformational', was drawn to illustrate different possibilities for the future library. Bell argued that 'traditional strategic planning may now be too constrained to properly respond to crisis and opportunity'. This was echoed by Stuart Hannabus when he criticised strategic planning as being too focused on the present to be an effective planning tool for a turbulent future.[33] The top-down, criterion-based approach and bureaucratic inflexibility inherent in traditional strategic planning does not help today's librarian to identify contingent decisions for unexpected changes or paradigm shifts in the information explosion age. On the other hand, the scenario development process enables conventional mindsets, existing strategies and people's competencies to be checked against various alternative scenarios. In a nutshell, the scenario approach enables managers 'to focus on opportunity-seeking planning rather than operations-driven planning'.[34]

Putting theories into practice, the Library of the University of Technology, Sydney applied the scenario planning process to achieve a shared understanding about its future direction.[35] The University of New South Wales Library, also in Sydney, employed the scenario modelling techniques for organis-ational restructuring, staff development, space planning and client services.[36] In the United States, the structured and disciplined techniques in developing plausible scenarios were employed at the Libraries of the University of Nebraska-Lincoln, to develop four possible futures to answer the question: 'How might the collection develop over the next five years?'[37] In Denmark, different stakeholders participated in scenario workshops to engage in 'strategic reflexive conversation' on three public library development projects.[38]

Regardless of the size of the library or where it is placed within its parent organisation, scenario planning can provide the stimulus necessary to direct it toward an imaginative thoughtful and stimulating future.

Notes

1. Bernstein, P. (2009). *Australian Financial Review*, 4–5 July, p. 40

2. The Open Access Movement is effectively an extension of the Open Source movement whereby programmes sought to create software that could be modified by all and not be proprietary. In a similar way libraries have commenced the Open Access movement to make as much literature as possible available freely on the Internet and not locked in proprietary publisher databases.

3. Meyrowitz, J. (1985). *No Sense of Place*. New York: Oxford University Press.

4. Legacy collections can be described in terms of the print never to be digitised because of copyright restriction and an inability to find the copyright owner. It represents a significant corpus of material.

5. Chown, M. (2008). 'Is science fiction dying?' *New Scientist*, 12 November, pp. 6–49.

6. Ibid. p. 47.

7. Skidelsky, R. (2008). 'No perfect knowledge out there in markets'. *China Daily (HK Edition)*, 31 December, p. 9.

8. Available at: *www2.ku.edu/~sfcenter/library.htm* (accessed 20 July 2010)

9. Clarke, A. C. (2008/2009). *Time*, 29 December/5 January, p. 96.

10. Gibbs, N. (2008). 'President-Elect Obama'. *Time*, 17 November, p. 25

11. Carr, N. (2008). *The Big Switch: rewiring the world, from Edison to Google*. NY: Norton, p. 228.

12. Markoff, J. (2008). 'Internet Traffic begins to bypass the US' *NY Times.com*, 31 August. Available at: *www.nytimes.com/2008/08/30/business/30pipes.html?scp=1&sq=Internet%20traffic%20bypasses%20us&st=cse* (accessed 31 August 2008).

13. Technorati (2009). *State of the Blogosphere 2009*, Available at: *http://technorati.com/blogging/feature/state-of-the-blogosphere-2009* (accessed 12 May 2010).

14. Ibid.

15. Schwartz, P. (1991). *The Art of the Long View*. New York: Doubleday Currency, pp. 3–4.

16. O'Connor, S. (2009). 'Beyond the Great Wall: Experiences with ETDs and open access in China and South East Asia'. Available at: *http://hdl.handle.net/10397/* (accessed 12 June 2009).

17. See, for example, *http://philb.com/fatesiks2.htm* (accessed 6 July 2009).

18. Christenson, C. M. (1997). *The Innovator's Dilemma: When new technologies cause great firms to fail* Boston, MA: Harvard Business School Press.

19. 'Can Judy McGrath keep MTV Networks up with the beat of the Internet era?' *The Economist*, 22 November 2008, p. 72.

20. Broder, J. N. (2009). 'Edward M. Kennedy, Senate Stalwart, is dead at 77'. *NY Times*, 27 August. Available at: *www.nytimes.com/2009/08/27/us/politics.* (accessed 28 August 2009).

21. Star, J. (2007). 'Growth scenarios: tools to resolve leaders' denial and paralysis.' *Strategy & Leadership* 35(2): pp. 56–9

22. Wright, G., van der Heijden, K., George, B., Bradfield, R. and Cairns, G. (2008). 'Scenario planning interventions in organisations: An analysis of the causes of success and failure.' *Futures* 40(3): pp. 218–36

23. Wack, P. (1985). 'Scenarios: shooting the rapids', *Harvard Business Review* 63(6): 139–50.

24. Cornelius, P., Van de Putte, A. and Romani, M. (2005). 'Three decades of scenario planning in Shell'. *California Management Review* 48(1): 92–109.

25. Weinstein, B. (2007). 'Scenario planning: current state of the art.' *Manager Update* 18 (3): 1.

26. Chermack, T. J. (2008). 'Scenario planning: Human resource development's strategic learning tool.' *Advances in Developing Human Resources* 10(2): 129–46.

27. Korte, R. F. and Chermack, T. J. (2007). 'Changing organisational culture with scenario planning.' *Futures* 39(6): 645–56.

28. Bradfield, R., Wright, G., Burt, G., Cairns, G. and Van Der Heijden, K. (2005). 'The origins and evolution of scenario techniques in long range business planning.' *Futures* 37(8): 795–812

29. Lindgren, M. and Bandhold, H. (2005). *Scenario Planning: The link between future and strategy.* New York: Palgrave Macmillan.

30. Giesecke, J. (1998). *Scenario Planning for Libraries.* Chicago, IL: American Library Association.

31. Willmore, J. (2001). 'Scenario planning: creating strategy for uncertain times.' *Information Outlook* 5(9): 22–8.

32. Bell, S. J. (1999). 'Using the scenario approach for achieving sustainable development in academic libraries.' Available at: *www.ala.org/ala/acrl/acrlevents/bell99.pdf* (accessed 8 April 2008).

33. Hannabuss, S. (2001). 'Scenario planning for libraries.' *Library Management* 22(4/5): 168–76.

34. Richards, L., O'Shea, J. and Connolly, M. (2004). 'Managing the concept of strategic change within a higher education institution: the role of strategic and scenario planning techniques.' *Strategic Change* 13(7): 345–59.

35. O'Connor, S., Blair, L. and McConchie, P. (1997). 'Scenario planning for a library future.' *Australian Library Journal* 46(2): 186–94

36. Wells, A. (2007). 'A prototype twenty-first century university library.' *Library Management* 28(8/9): 450–9.

37. Giesecke, J. (1999). 'Scenario planning and collection development.' *Journal of Library Administration* 28(1): 81–92.

38. Kristiansson, M. R. (2007). 'Strategic reflexive conversation: a new theoretical-practice field within LIS.' Information Research 12(4). Available at: *http://informationr.net/ir/12-4/colis/colis18.html* (accessed 23 April 2008).

2

The complexities of our informational environment

This chapter

This chapter will examine the concept of the environment as a space in which each of our libraries exists. It will also enable the reader to see the environment for what it is while also analysing, and then beginning to understand, the impacts of the environment. There are various tools which will assist us in these examinations.

By examining the environment we will then have the basis by which to understand, in a subsequent chapter, the business models operating in the publishing and library industries.

What is the environment?

Geologists and sociologists understand our physical and social environments. They understand the contours, the seismic shifts, the changes in attitudes, the movement of populations and social classes. The development of their disciplines involves gathering information from a variety of information sources and integrating them to provide new information. These two disciplines have much in common with the library and information profession.

The geologist and the sociologist have differences, however, in how they can garner facts from their environments. The geologist can rely on observations and investigations about the earth and geological movements. The sociologist knows that there are constant changes in the social order. Attitudes change and there are so many factors which influence the shape of society. Societal changes can be measured and tracked with quantitative and qualitative measures.

Libraries and their environments

The environment in which our libraries operate varies from sector to sector. The environment in which a special library operates is different to that for a public library or an academic library. They differ because of the funding, administrative and political influences. They differ because of the salary scales on offer to their staffs and also, at a more fundamental level, because of their missions and the populations which they intend to serve. These environments need to be understood and to be gauged as to what they are telling us about the possible futures for their libraries. We will talk more about how to deal with these environments later in this chapter.

The wider environments are often more difficult to see and understand but are nonetheless critical to establishing an understanding of what is possible, what is probable and why we need to change our thinking. But there are seismic shifts occurring in each of these environments and it is important to be aware of them and to appreciate, at least broadly, what they mean. The geologist would be concerned that the moving tectonic plates might upset the very foundations of the cities above them. These are the insights which will more strongly drive the scenarios which are developed in later chapters.

Anything's possible if you've got enough nerve. (J.K. Rowling[1])

Disruptive technologies

It is worthwhile now talking about 'disruptive technologies'. This is a business theory popularised by Clayton M. Christensen to describe how a new technology can affect existing technologies, particularly if it is unexpected. In his 1997 best-selling book, *The Innovator's Dilemma*, Christensen separates new technology into two categories: sustaining and disruptive. Sustaining technology relies on incremental improvements to an already established technology. Disruptive technology lacks refinement, often has performance problems because it is new, appeals to a limited audience, and may not yet have a proven practical application. (Such was the case with Alexander Graham Bell's 'electrical speech machine', which we now call the telephone.) In his book, Christensen points out that large corporations are designed to work with sustaining technologies. They excel at knowing their market, staying close to their customers, and having a mechanism in place to develop existing technology. Conversely, they have trouble capitalising on the potential efficiencies, cost-savings, or new marketing opportunities created by low-margin disruptive technologies. Using real-world examples to illustrate his point, Christensen demonstrates how 'it is not unusual for a big corporation to dismiss the value of a disruptive technology because it does not reinforce current company goals, only to be blindsided as the technology matures, gains a larger audience and market share, and threatens the status quo'.[2] More recent and relevant examples for libraries might relate to the emergence of the personal computer (PC), for instance. This was a hugely disruptive technology to the mainframe computer company IBM, who were dismissive that the humble PC would ever have any impact. They were complacent. In fact it 'destroyed' their central mainframe computing business. Bill Gates became a very rich man through the conversion of the IBM code into

MS-DOS, a version suitable for the personal computer. It also created the software giant Microsoft. This story is detailed in the book *Hard Drive*.[3] It is as Christensen observes: the large corporation could not see how the PC would fit into their business model and as a result of this, the PC destroyed their mass market business model. It is also useful to note that the PC had a wide-ranging effect on the rise of the 'individual': we could easily work on our own, in isolation from others and remote from the offices where IBM had us tied. The PC was a disruption with a manifold impact. 'What if' the PC had never happened? Can you imagine this? In the same way, in the next chapter we will look into the past in order to begin to see the future.

Another disruptive technology is the mobile phone. The mobile phone is now replacing the paper diary and book of contacts (the paper diary itself had already been disrupted by the PDA device such as the Palm), and is also disrupting the camera (the film camera had been replaced by the digital camera). So into the one compact device, the functions of diary, contacts, camera and now music storage and player are combined with the common function of a telephone. Businesses specialising in any one of the earlier technologies such as paper diaries manufacturers and distributors, camera manufacturing companies such as Kodak, and makers of cassette or record music players have all been disrupted in a very short space of time. The mobile phone continues to evolve to provide access to a host of information resources including, for example OCLC's (the very large 'consortium' company providing bibliographic data to libraries) enormous catalogue, WorldCat, with its access to collections of more than 10,000 libraries worldwide.

The exercise accompanying this chapter will assist you to identify disruptive technologies and to examine their impact or their potential impact.

Broad disruptive technological impact on libraries

Assuming a broad understanding of the concept of disruptive technologies, it is now worthwhile thinking about the impact of digital technology on libraries.

In the mid 1990s it became possible for the first time to commercially deliver digital content via the Internet. Prior to this, digital content was restricted to the storage media of the CD (compact disc) and emerging into more compact but similar media. This was a huge move away from the microfiche as a storage medium. But even the additional capacity of the CD quickly became a problem and we saw the emergence of CD jukeboxes to cope with the number of CDs which were becoming necessary to store the content and the need to get to the relevant CD as quickly as possible. Of course, the CD's data capacity quickly increased through the creation of dual-layered DVDs, making the CD jukeboxes themselves redundant.

The advent of *digital delivery* of content has had a profound disruptive impact on the library. The extent of this impact is, in many ways, not yet fully realised. With the growth of the capability of the Internet to deliver digital content to libraries it became possible for library users to use the library without even accessing the physical library building. This changing demographic of the library population is not a passing phenomenon but a growing one, leading to reduced turnstile counts. Fewer people are coming through the library doors, but paradoxically the use of the library is increasing and is increasing manifold. The physical library building is often turning to purposes other than the original model. There are coffee shops and community centres, and we have performance areas and retail outlets within the old library fabric. None of this is necessarily wrong but it is important that the library and information centre has a clear idea of where the organisation is heading as well as its purpose. Unfortunately, however, we have many libraries 'losing their way' as they struggle to find their raison d'être.

Digital delivery is fundamentally changing and disrupting the position of the library in its community. It is sometimes the case that the library is perceived by those communities to be irrelevant. It is openly wondered 'why do we need a library when we have the Internet?' While digital content is delivered to the user's desktop via the Internet, the user can easily be forgiven when they do not even realise that the service is coming from the library via subscriptions. The users do not have, in this situation, any conception that the service takes a lot of organisation and that it does cost money, a lot of real money. The Internet is not providing access to this information at no cost. So the disruptive technology of *digital delivery* is and will continue to have a profound effect.

Library staff will, in this environment, not easily understand this impact. If their work is in the process of acquiring, collecting and making this digital content accessible, they will not easily recognise that their work has changed markedly. The impact on the whole organisation will be profound. The nature of their work in making content available digitally is changing. They are no longer working with 'tactile' information such as books and bound serials. Their work is largely unseen as the product of their work, digital content, is disconnected from the physical library. If the staff work in information services they will need to recognise the very fundamental change that many of their users are unseen to them. They are users in the virtual environment. If users are remote, staff will need a very profound change in their thinking and behaviours if they are to understand the information needs of these unseen users.

These responses should be in terms of appropriate services and in terms of collection development. The 'disruptive technology' impact on collection development is one of the most important issues we face as we commence the

---

Exercise

What are 'disruptive technological' impacts? Here we can see how various 'technologies' change the way in which any business is and can be done. This exercise is meant to examine disruptive technologies near and then in libraries.

Part 1

1. Consider what has happened to the paper diary? Has it been replaced by the Personal Diary Assistant (PDA)?
2. Consider the classic film camera company Kodak. Did it react to the emergence of digital or fail to react quickly enough?
3. What impact has the Internet had on the delivery of information content for libraries?

Part 2

1. What has been the impact on the paper diary industry? Has it or will it survive?
2. Kodak was dominant in this camera manufacturing industry; it has not been a strong player at all in the digital world.
3. Has 'digital delivery' of content fundamentally changed the way in which libraries do business?

---

twenty-first century. What we collect and make available to a largely unseen user population creates in itself many challenges, both intellectual and procedural. These impacts aside, the greatest effect of this is on the library staff, their work patterns, and their perceptions of the need to change organisational patterns, work behaviours and work design. These staff issues will be developed in a later chapter.

Issues in the wider environment

There are many issues shadowing the library environment which are having an impact on what can and cannot be achieved. The issues which are being explored in this chapter impact on all library sectors, in all geographic areas of the world. Invariably they are issues we should be aware of as they will impact on our future planning decisions and on the thinking, indeed rethinking, of all library and information services. It may well be that libraries will not be able to respond to or influence some or all of these issues and in some senses, this does not matter. What is critical, however, is that we understand what is broadly happening in our environment because only then can we decide with greater certainty where to take our strategic positions; where to point our strategies.

Open source

Bill Gates demonstrated great foresight and was indeed lucky to make MS-DOS code the operating system of the very early personal computers (PCs). The PC is now a very sophisticated machine but still the basic code or sets of instruction are proprietary. This DOS code, along with the software behind most of the major computer systems (Fortran, Sun and so on) is known as proprietary source code. Computer code directs the computer how to operate as a set of instructions. Proprietary code locks those instructions so that they cannot be changed without the permission of the software owner. History has rarely seen this type of situation, where crucial developments can be locked away. If we all worked solely on our own without connection to other people it might not have mattered. But this is not the case. We are very connected to each other locally and internationally. The extent to which we can connect or innovate with others is very dependent on what our computer systems will allow us. Proprietary systems are good if we never wish to change anything or if the manufacturer or software owner had unlimited capacity to change at ease. As the world is changing rapidly then software systems must also change at the same rate. Proprietary systems are dinosaurs for any innovating service. They are not responsive to connectivity or change. Because integrated library systems (ILS) have been written using proprietary code, the ILS as a library tool is closed, locked as an exclusively proprietary system. It has therefore been quite difficult to get any ILS to talk to other systems without great cost being involved. The systems are also expensive to develop as each system owner has to pay for the development of their own system including common elements. There has been a consolidation of these systems over recent years for a variety of reasons. In the 1980s there would have been more than ten main ILS vendors in the market. Nowadays there would be no more than four systems. It is a shrinking market. Among the reasons has been the entry of private equity companies into the library markets, generally attracted by the very solid and reliable cash flows. This entry has not seen the costs to the library decrease.

In many senses the world turns in circles. In the late 1970s library systems existed for two prime purposes: to automate and make cataloguing services more efficient and to operate circulation systems. A number of these modules were developed by one library or another and shared, for little or no cost, with other libraries. The story of these developments is a fascinating tale in itself; a story of great innovation and vision. Realising the viability of this new industry, library automation companies came into existence to develop the full suite of library service modules. But they developed as proprietary systems as this was the only way the software at the time allowed and of course for the profit motive as well. Now systems such as *LibLime* are hitting the market as Open Source systems, encouraging the free availability of cataloguing records as well. OCLC have also announced the release of their web-based ILS. The vision is to avoid each library maintaining its own software and server and rather relying on a central system (or OCLC) operating across the Internet, in the cloud as it were, making a host of other inter-linked systems possible. At the same time OCLC are also seeking to tighten their 'ownership' of the records in WorldCat from further commercial use, so they will not lose future potential income. So the advent and growing popularity of 'open source' is beginning to have wider impacts.

> Open Source software ... permits users to use, change, and improve the software, and to redistribute it in modified or unmodified form. It is very often developed in a public, collaborative manner. Open source software is the most prominent example of open source development and often compared to user generated content.[4]

Linux is one prominent example of open source software which has gained widespread popularity. Open source enables users to develop software, to share it and to grow the capability of the computer programs without having to pay, and pay for upgrades. This sharing and collaborative mode is a fundamental characteristic of the Internet. The development of applications which can be shared between libraries and information services, enabling them to offer more innovative and effective services, is a new way of working. Equally, while libraries have had a strong and undisputed role in our society over the past number of centuries, this may not always be the case. The concepts espoused by Google to organise the information or to create digital copies of all the world's literature could readily be seen to be 'library concepts'. The point being made above is that proprietary systems have locked innovative development in libraries. The freeing up of the software through open source developments is an opportunity for libraries but it is also an opening for others to usurp the traditional role of libraries. The opportunity to innovate is not only for libraries but for anyone.

Open source is also now playing into the emergence of Web 2.0 initiatives. If Web 1.0 encapsulated the effective delivery of html documents to users, Web 2.0 is seeking to enable user participation through the capability of the Internet. It is providing software to enable interactivity of users to users, of users to information and of the effective interchange of information and user need across the vehicle of the Internet. So the conjunction of open source and Web 2.0 poses significant opportunities for libraries to position their services for greater effect.

If this book concerns itself with the future then we must consider the future development of the web, the influence of open source and the emergence of the Semantic Web. Web 3.0 could be described as Web 2.0 being driven by the Semantic Web and other emerging influences. If the traditional web presents information in our natural language, to be interpreted by humans and not machines, then the Semantic Web is the natural extension, having computers filtering and organising information with the direction of humans. The classic article by the founder of the World Wide Web, Tim Berners-Lee,[5] on the Semantic Web is well worth reading. 'The Semantic Web is not a separate Web but an extension of the current one, in which information is given well-defined meaning, better enabling computers and people to work in cooperation. The first steps in weaving the Semantic Web into the structure of the existing Web are already under way. In the near future, these developments will usher in significant new functionality as machines become much better able to process and "understand" the data that they merely display at present.'[6] Libraries are well positioned to design and inform these systems, perhaps in partnership with designers and innovators. Library staffs were composed until recently almost exclusively of professional, para-professional librarians and clerical staff. Now and increasingly, there will be other professional disciplines such as database managers, web designers, marketing managers, curriculum designers and event organisers. Diversity of employment types will be the key to getting the most effective library organisation. In this way, librarian skills will be more sharply defined and focused.

Open source implications

There are a number of implications flowing from the wide availability of open source solutions. Firstly, there is the move which is seeing more open source computer applications being available in the marketplace. This in turn is allowing for the 'democratisation' of software applications. Libraries in this environment can watch out for community developed software which might suit their information distribution needs.

Secondly, with the emergence of open source ILSs, libraries may consider the future of their proprietary library systems and the costs associated with them. In a time when the emphases are changing from the collection being physically bound to the library building to one where the collection is most significantly digital in nature and widely available, the library will have to consider where they place their systems development. It will almost certainly not be with the traditional ILS acquiring, storing and circulating physical items. The emphasis will need to be on innovative, inventive access and discovery tools for the digital collections and the need to work more and more on the Internet. If the traditional catalogue has been a 'pull' technology, then what the library needs is more 'push' technologies. A 'pull' technology is a static technology. It is there for people to use at their own need or pace. A 'push' technology can anticipate an information need and push the information to a user. An example of this might be where a library has created a profile of every library user's information interests. With this profile, news of the annual of a new book relevant to a profile could be 'pushed' to the user.

Thirdly, if Web 1.0 existed to connect users and html documents, Web 2.0 is creating the interactivity between users and information with applications, often open sourced to enable and heighten that interconnectivity. Web 3.0 will see the development of the Semantic Web on the foundations of Web 2.0 initiatives but it will be driven by computers gathering and organising information according to the information needs of humans. What will the future role for libraries be in that environment? Will individual libraries or local library systems have the resources, let alone the capability, to compete with this technological advance?

Digital content

As the volume of information available on the Internet has burgeoned, growing at exponential rates, so too have the costs and copyright implications of the availability of this information become an issue. Traditional publishers, in making the content of their books and journals available on the Internet, have sought to ensure that their business model is sustainable. In moving away from a print-based business model where revenue flows and profit margins were known and reliable, they have embraced digital publishing but have sought guarantees for the future of their business operations. They have locked up the content for the lifetime of their authors plus 70 years.[7] In addition, as they have seen the impact of digital availability they have made the retrospective collections also available in digital form, effectively putting this content under license arrangements where the user has to pay to gain access. The main legal issue in the future library operating environment will not be copyrights but licensing. The availability of print will stabilise at a low percentage of library collection while all the digital content will be licensed. The licensing conditions will be very definitive and restrictive, allowing for little shaping of content. The digital popularity of older content has been described by Chris Anderson, the editor of *Wired*, as the long tail.[8] Effectively the theory and indeed the experience has been that, if you make older content available in digital form, it will be sought and retrieved by users. This observation is also a significant driver behind Google Books.[9]

As discussed in the *Open Source* section above, the emergence of the Open Access movement has presented challenges to both traditional publishers and librarians. Open access advocates argue that publicly funded research or writing should be publicly available as soon as possible. With a number of publishers, the compromise between commercial return on the investment in the original publishing and the commitment to open access is to make their content openly available six to nine months after publication. Still, these publishers are in the minority. The major publishers still lock their content behind firewalls and will no doubt continue to do so for the foreseeable future. Some publishers have adapted an open access stance that will allow immediate open access for an article if the article has been paid to be published, typically paid by the author. This cost is typically around US$2,500. This 'pay to publish' model in Western publishing will still have the imprimatur of peer reviewed acceptance. Chinese publishing already has both business models operating side-by-side. There is great pressure in Chinese universities to publish to achieve promotion. There is the capacity, however, to pay to publish without the quality stamp of 'peer review'. Changes in this publishing paradigm will only happen with changes in attitude by the academic community as to where they wish to publish. Another key factor in this change will be how universities measure their quality outcomes. If they continue to use measures such as impact factors and citation analyses, they will strive to publish only in those journals which are perceived to have the greatest quality and prestige. This will have the effect of both renewing the same range of journals and also increasing subscription rates. So the drivers of the success of open access will lie significantly with the academic community, the drivers of peer review, perceived quality and competition between universities.

Digital content implications

The nature of digital content is having significant impact on library information tools, and will continue to do so into the future. Firstly, digital content is invariably favoured by the vast majority of library users, as they can access the information from *anywhere and everywhere*. This situation requires sophisticated proxy server environments in order to be able to deliver the digital content to the library's defined community.

Secondly, the increasing availability of digital content on the Internet, through Google Books and other services, is highlighting that most of the world's publishing content *may* be accessible across the Internet at some stage into our future. This will severely affect the role of the library and its *raison d'être* in the eyes of both users and funding bodies.

Thirdly, digital content from publishers will continue to exist and will represent the bulk of content provided through subscription or purchase, to library users.

Finally, the Open Access movement is building momentum to encourage the free availability of published literature on the Internet. This will impact the library–publisher relationship in three ways: it will encourage publishers to make the published versions of their material freely available after say an embargo of six to twelve months; it has and will continue to open the possibility of libraries becoming publishers in their own right; and it fundamentally changes the relationship between the author and the publisher. The issue of authenticity and credibility in published texts will be key in the future of this issue.

The author–publisher–library relationship

To understand scholarly publishing it is essential to look at the relationship between the author, the publisher and the

Figure 2.1 Traditional publishing model

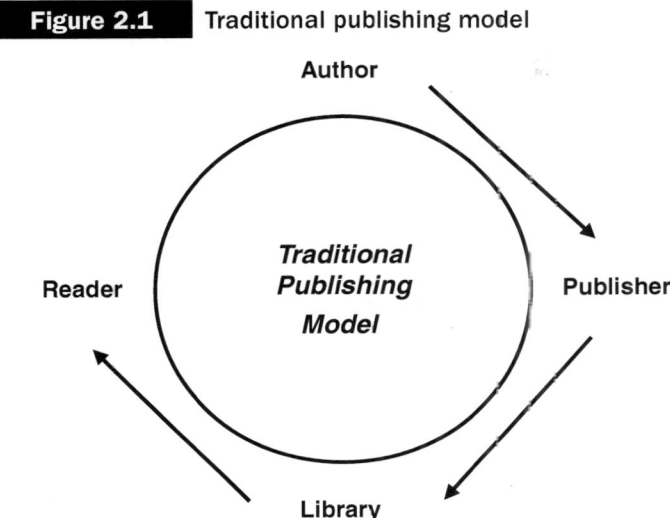

Source: Steve O'Connor

library. The interplay is crucially important. In the traditional scholarly publishing model the author seeks a publisher and a journal and the library funds the journal for the reader. It is encapsulated in the circulate model above.

This effectively has been the business model for the traditional publisher. The advent of the Internet has offered the publisher new business models to go directly to the reader and bypass the library. These new business models are critical to their commercial process. This will be discussed further in Chapter 3.

Content balance

Already the nature of the content being collected by each library is changing. Digital content became available on CDs in the late 1980s and gradually via the Internet in the early 1990s. So libraries began collecting their content in digital form and the amount of print material fell. It has, in certain library systems, continued to fall. But what is the mix now and what is it likely to be in a few short years? Whatever mix is now evident, each library system will shape the type of building and facilities which are required; will shape the computer/Internet infrastructure which is required; will shape the budget which is required; will shape the staff skills which are required; and most importantly, will shape the perception which a library's users have of that library service and its future. In a similar way, the different disciplines served by the library will have different informational needs. They will each have different delivery mechanisms. Science and technology disciplines will most likely have their information delivered via on-line journals; social sciences and humanities will have a mix of e-journals and e-books as well as print books.

Exercise

What will be the mix of content coming into your library?

Understanding what is happening to the types of content being acquired for the library will have huge implications for how your library development is being planned.

Part 1

1. Assess as closely as possible the percentage of resources available to your library's users.
2. Using the chart in Figure 2.2, determine what is the percentage of print acquisitions coming into your library now? What is the percentage of digital resources acquired through subscription? What is the percentage of information gained through access to the information resources on the Internet?

3. What impact has the Internet had on the delivery of information content for libraries?

4. Predict the percentages coming into the library over a ten-year period. Do this as individuals and examine the resulting work as a group.

Part 2

1. The mixture of content predictec by different individuals will often vary wildly and is a good point of discussion.

2. The predictions over a ten-year pericd will often be wrong in two respects:
   (a) the change will happen a lot earlier and
   (b) the changes will be greater than predicted.

3. This exercise is well worth doing and 'putting in the bottom drawer' to see how your views change over time, even over the space of one year.

4. This exercise is also worth doing for different purposes. It may be for budget predictions. It may be for future staff or skill resource needs.

Figure 2.2   Library content mix

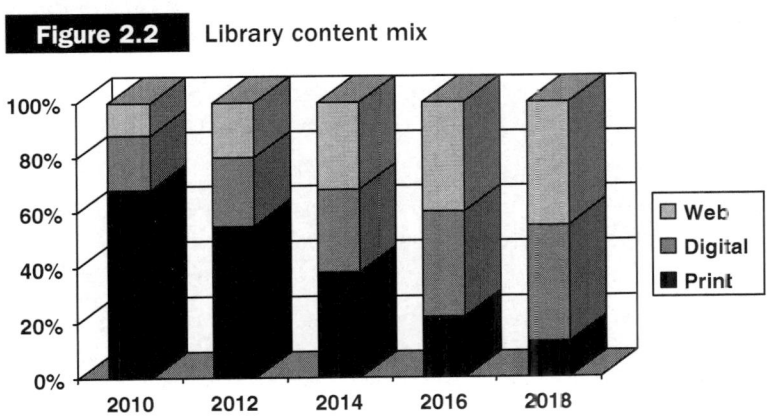

Source: Steve O'Connor

The future of work

In preparing for the future we have to consider the future organisation. This is the vehicle through which the future scenarios are to be delivered. Invariably, organisations are shaped by the tools they have to deliver the organisation's mission. Large organisations can be very difficult to change as they have perceptions of their aim, role or position which are largely directed toward self-sustenance. A large organisation with large powerful departments can find change almost impossible to achieve. Yet small companies with the new computer tools and the availability of the Internet can have a far greater impact than their size indicates. They can create niche businesses where there was no opportunity before. A small start-up can be more nimble, progressive and swift than a large bureaucracy. The nature of work and work patterns are helping this to occur. They are also driven by the skills of their people.

The point, mentioned earlier in this book, that IBM completely missed the disruptive influence of the personal computer is a key observation to understanding the issue of work. In designing work flows, the PC is still supreme and a large expenditure item in the capital and maintenance budgets of our libraries. The financial tsunami of late 2008 and early 2009 will have work implications for many years to come. Apart from placing pressure on the availability of work, it will also sharply impact on the way in which we actually work; it will heighten new ways of work being organised for groups or as individuals. Businesses surrounding our library will re-examine their existing operations for effectiveness and profitability while new businesses will also emerge from the opportunities created by this severe economic downturn. The issues raised earlier in this chapter and indeed in Chapter 1 have highlighted the seismic shifts in the patterns of information delivery. If the major uses of the library service are occurring remotely, then how should we respond? Do we focus on what we know best, do we race and change everything, do we engage partners, do we encourage others to deliver certain services while we focus on other areas?

Implications for the future of work

The disruptive technologies mentioned earlier in this chapter will have a strong effect on the shape of the resulting library organisation. It is a matter of 'seeing' these changes and trying to understand their likely impact. Organisations today are clearly not as hierarchical as they were, say, twenty years ago. There is an openness to their operation and decision-making. Some describe this as self-organising, consensus decision-making, empowerment, democratic, even flattened organisational structures. There is a greater degree of participative decision-making in the workplace. But in what direction is the workplace now going? The Internet poses opportunities for staff to work away from the organisation's theoretical headquarters. To work at home has realised many advantages and cost savings to the organisation but has created other problems such as a diffusion to the organisation's purpose and direction as well as personal isolation. Still, this trend to off-site or at home work is a reality and has to be assessed as to how it can be used in one's organisation. The Internet also shapes the nature of the work we do and therefore the way in which we organise ourselves. John Malone, in his book *The Future of Work*, argues for the various models of organisation on a continuum from independence, through centralisation, to decentralisation. A common experience in public and academic libraries over the past ten to fifteen years has been the merger of local councils and higher education institutions and the resulting impacts on previously independent libraries. Will economic pressures force the larger organisational units, to which libraries invariably belong, to seek to remove middle management and to aggregate smaller units to achieve perceived efficiencies? These trends have been common over the past twenty years and are not likely to disappear in the near future. Independence still exists for libraries, notably special libraries, but for all of us, there is a far greater sense of strategic inter-dependence. Even those libraries which exist within centralised systems experience the inter-dependence of their system with other systems. The diagrams below are modelled on the work of John Malone but are just as effectively applied to our library environment.

Independent libraries

Independent libraries exist without much connection to each other. Invariably they exist in an environment in which they might accede to certain standards of performance (e.g. MARC records) but otherwise have separate, autonomous existences,

Figure 2.3   Independent libraries

Source: Steve O'Connor

organisational hierarchies and strategic imperatives. Some of these libraries may also have branch libraries but the systems are theoretically independent.

Centralised library

The centralised library exists where systems are larger and more complex but where there is far less scope for independence of the member libraries within such systems. Each of the libraries owes its existence and funding to the central operation. Even in this model each of the libraries can maintain some degree of autonomy and proud independence. But, in the end analysis, they have to work with the centre because without resources they will wither.

Networked libraries

The new networked or Internet level of connectiveness has opened new ways of organisations working to achieve their outcomes.

Figure 2.4 Centralised libraries

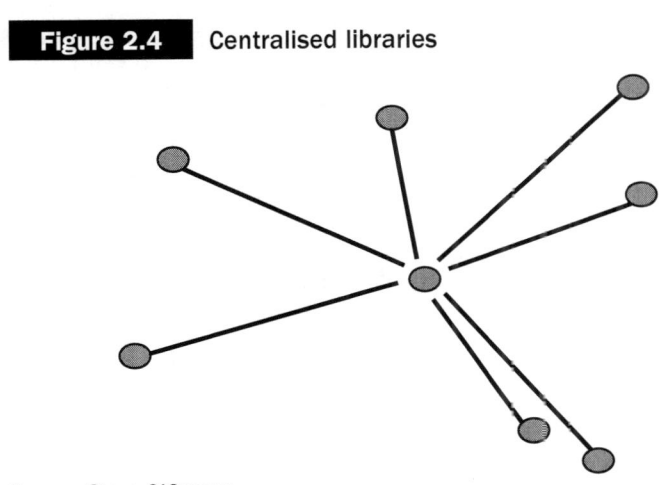

Source: Steve O'Connor

It is into this networked, connected world that libraries will find themselves moving more and more. The style of management used in a hierarchical, independent environment will be very different from the management style which will be needed to be effective in a networked or consortium environment. The managers who are used to being in charge in their home environment will need to adopt much more consensual approaches as they work with peers from other library systems. Complicating matters is that the peers in a networked environment will not necessarily be from libraries of equal resource dimensions and yet they will carry equal influence in this new environment. Even the largest libraries need the support of the smallest libraries in this networked environment if they are to succeed. Examples of this are where physical resources are shared across different library systems, so that the user gains the advantage. All library partners in such a situation gain advantage, politically and operationally. Library users do not care where the resource comes from. This is especially the case where the

Figure 2.5 Networked libraries

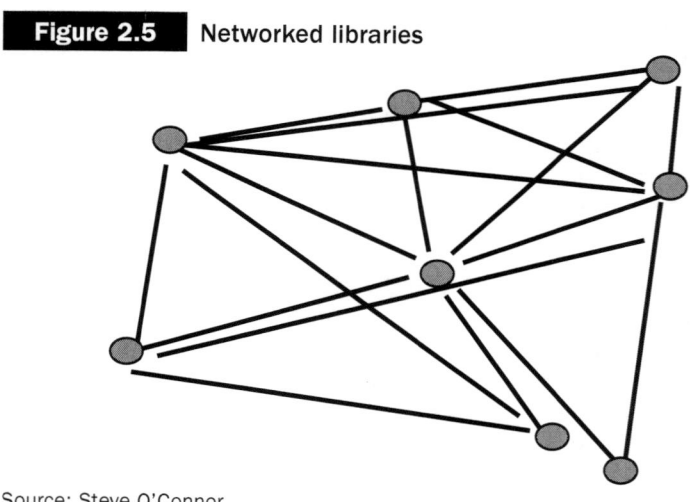

Source: Steve O'Connor

service operates across the Internet. The outcome which is transparent to the end user is the delivered information product whether it is a physical book or a digital information package.

The number of consortium organisations in the library world today will steadily diminish over the next ten years, but they will be more powerful organisations carrying significant responsibilities for the libraries in their membership in this networked world. Consortia organisations are not a library invention but their role and character is peculiarly suited to the library and information environment.

In the world of library and information services there are many different organisations which are tagged as a 'consortium'. These will range from local groups established to assist groups of libraries to work together, to one such as OhioLINK, which was established to assist libraries in the state of Ohio, USA to spend state and university funds to purchase datasets together. Some organisations such as CAVAL, Victoria, Australia were established to provide cooperative cataloguing and then grew to a number of other functions including cooperative storage of low-use research materials. OCLC is the largest of all 'consortia' although it is difficult to agree that, at a turnover of over US$50 million each year, it is actually a humble consortium. SOLINET is a genuine consortium with over 3,000 library members spanning an increasing range of states in the USA. The trend, already mentioned, is that there will be a consolidation of consortia. PALINET and NELINET have now merged with SOLINET to form the new group LYRASIS.

It is not intended in this chapter to detail all consortia, their nature, governance and purpose: suffice it to say that the consortium is a legal device to enable libraries to work together to achieve a common purpose.

Emerging trends

If anyone were to doubt the power and utility of the Internet, the inauguration of Barack Obama as the 44th President of the United States provides a few salutary lessons. 'Ratings show that the January 20 inauguration was the first time that more people tuned in to a live, high-profile event on the Internet than on television.'[10] But in this context, what are the issues which matter to your own library?

Exercise

What are the emerging issues for you and your library? Each library will operate in its own peculiar environment with its own pressures. The emerging issues listed in this chapter will be useful, but only as a guide.

Part 1

1. What are the pressures which your parent organisation is currently dealing with?
2. What issues does your organisation believe will be important in three years' time?
3. Does your organisation think and behave strategically?

Part 2

1. It is worthwhile listing and then grouping the issues and to attempt to place priority to them from the patent organisation point of view and then from the perspective of the library.

Later chapters will examine techniques by which the future can be assessed and, to the extent possible, managed. However, looking at libraries at this point in time, a generalisation could be made that the average age of staff would be quite high. If this is the case then a number of observations would follow.

Firstly, there are many potential employment and progression opportunities opening up. Secondly, the current leadership may be finding it difficult to relate to and understand the needs and outlooks of the younger user, and indeed staff. Generational change brings its challenges but also its prospects for new insights and contributions. In this situation the existing leadership and the new library generations have a mutual benefit in truly listening to each other and, of course, to their users. We now have a new young President in the United States holding the prospects of new ways of dealing with the future.

This chapter has examined the main trends affecting libraries as they decide on their future directions. The emphases and the detail will be different for each and every library system. Later chapters will build on this work.

Notes

1. Rowling, J. K. (2007). *Harry Potter and the Order of the Phoenix.* As cited in *http://www.quotationspage.com/quote/33790.html* (accessed on 14 February 2010).
2. Available at: *http://whatis.techtarget.com/definition/0,,sid9_gci945822,00.html* (accessed on 6 February 2009).
3. Wallace, J. and Erickson, J. (1992). *Hard Drive: Bill Gates and the making of the Microsoft empire.* New York: Wiley.
4. Open Source Software. Available at: *http://en.wikipedia.org/wiki/Open-source_software* (accessed on 11 February 2009).

5. Berners-Lee, T. (2001). 'The semantic web' *Scientific American*, 17 May. Available at: *www.sciam.com/article.cfm?id=the-semantic-web&print=true* (accessed on 15 February 2009).
6. Ibid.
7. The period of 70 years has only recently been extended from 50 years under international copyright law. It is likely to be extended further into the future.
8. Anderson, C. (2006). *The Long Tail: Why the future of business is selling less of more*. New York: Hyperion.
9. Google Books is a major project to digitise much of the world's print books in cooperation with many of the world's largest and best libraries. There are similar projects emanating from many large library collections, such as the New York Public Library.
10. 'TV industry needs to log into the future' *South China Morning Post* LXV(33): B10 (4 February 2009).

3

The future and the past: models are changing

This chapter

This chapter will introduce you to the future through the vehicle of the past. In doing this we can begin to get a feeling of how we have seen the future and how often this is without a framework or understanding. We are now using tools which will help us establish horizons to the future. In looking from the past we can see that consortia have played a much stronger role and will do so into the future. We will also look at what the business model means to libraries and especially if we are expecting changes to the library's operations through this scenario process.

The mirror as a powerful tool

The mirror is a personal tool used to help us understand the reality of what we are rather than the perception we may think of ourselves. In this way, it tells us of the real world. It can be cruel; it can be kind depending on our own understanding of what or who we are.

The *rear vision mirror* is also a powerful tool used, as it is mostly, in a motor vehicle to reflect where we have been.

To extend the analogy, what we see in the rear vision mirror is an image of a time past. It may be of only the very recent past but it is of the time past ... where we have been already. It is far more difficult but it is really interesting to go back to where the rear vision mirror sees that we have been and to look forward. If we were able to go back to that past point and look forward we would be able to see the future. Many a science fiction writer has sought to create this capability, enabling us to visit different time periods and to see both into the past and into the future. So the rear vision mirror is a very useful instrument for us to begin to understand our past, our present and through this to our future.

As we discussed in Chapter 1, history is not linear but our progress from Point A to Point B is littered with decision points and obstacles which cause us to go in different directions. It is always difficult to see a situation in the future. But we can look

Figure 3.1 Rear vision mirror

Source: This image is used with the kind permission of David Hobbs. http://hobbsie.smugmug.com.

at it through the rear vision mirror. If we were to look back in our lives, we can remember how we felt and thought about certain events in our past lives. So it is for events in our professional lives. We can draw into our minds what we were thinking at the time as we remember when we first became aware of a computerised version of the card catalogue; when we became aware of the first personal computer being available in a library; when we first became aware that the Internet would be able to present digital content for the library; when we became aware that library content could be delivered digitally to a library's clientele no matter where they were located. By casting our minds back to that moment and remembering, from that perspective we can begin to understand how we saw the future at that time. We can understand our often 'inadequate' view of the future from one of those present moments. Looking back will also enable us to recollect the various choices which had been made to get us to the present moment. Yet remembering how we thought in that past time, the path to the future might have been considered linear. As we reflect on that past moment, we begin to see all of the characteristics in that situation which may have led to the future developments. When journal articles commenced being distributed on compact disc (CD), it was soon evident that this was a very welcome development. However, the volume of content was soon overwhelming the delivery vehicle ... the humble but relatively new technology the CD. The characteristics to recognise at that point were twofold: one, that the delivery of content via digital means was going to be the future path; secondly, there would need to be new technological devices to deliver that content. In planning terms it is not necessary for us to identify what the technology might be but to recognise that the direction was becoming clear. Plan for digital delivery. Plan for mass delivery of content. By extension, plan for the gradual transfer of much content into digital form.

Exercise

What is the Rear Vision Mirror Tool? It is difficult to predict the future but as we think back to a particular development we can remember what we thought of the development at the time and remember what we imagined of the future again at that time.

Part 1

1. Consider when you first saw a microfiche catalogue. What did you think about it at that time?
2. Was it the first time in which the catalogue could be present on all floors of the library and in offices across the organisation?

Part 2

1. Remembering how you felt at the time about this development, did you foresee the development of the online catalogue?
2. What are the existing technologies in the library and how might they be replaced or made redundant?
3. What were the impacts of this technological change which was different to the technology being replaced (i.e. the card catalogue)?
4. Did this change begin to impact on the nature and need for the physical library building?

Library models in transition

A library is a library is a library. At least this is the way it used to be. Libraries would collect and service, relating to their native client group while retaining their independence in all respects. In the past 40 years that natural order of things has begun to change with the emergence of umbrella groups to assist the libraries to achieve greater orders of efficiency and effectiveness. Most often, as the next section indicates, this was to achieve greater technological benefit. As the power of computers especially has increased they have also become smaller and more local, not normally requiring great central computer grunt. There are a few notable exceptions. An umbrella group became a consortium and now we have many consortia across the globe. But what is and will be the intersection mark between the two types of organisation?

Consortia in our corporate lives

An integral aspect of the life of the modern library is its relationship to one or more library consortia. Each library will belong to at least one consortium while many libraries will belong to many consortia. There has been an abundance of these organisations to assist libraries achieve different objectives or services. It is interesting to use the 'rear vision mirror' tool to see where consortia have come from and perhaps begin to understand their future role and that of the library's relationship to them.

The major consortia which came into existence in the 1960s did so, primarily, to operate union catalogues. Organisations such as BLCMP, OCLC and CAVAL established union catalogue operations to reduce member cataloguing operational costs by maintaining union catalogues and providing copy cataloguing facilities.

It is one thing to say that these union catalogues were established and operated. It is also worth reflecting on the huge changes and impacts which they had on library operations and staffs. Cataloguing departments in each organisation were previously independent from similar units in other organisations. With the creation and spread of the union catalogues, cataloguing departments were now increasingly connected and their practices became more and more uniform. The rear vision mirror tool may have foreseen the gradual but certain demise of the numbers of professional staff members in cataloguing departments.

In a similar but certain way, it is becoming increasingly obvious that cataloguing departments will merge into regional entities. If this is the case, the role of the library consortia will have again significantly altered the future of library members and their staffs. This is an interesting example of where a technological change has fundamentally changed a significant part of the library profession and certainly the way in which practice occurs in libraries. It has been a gradual but fundamental change; one that is not reversible. The practice of cataloguing, its standards and rules might have changed for ever but the utter importance of good clean data has not changed. This legacy will continue through the practice of the profession.

Various consortia spawned by OCLC, including SOLINET, PALINET, AMIGOS, NELINET and so on came into existence to support and market the central services of OCLC in geographic areas. Gradually each of these organisations took on other roles for their members. They also established themselves with their own governance. Looking backwards, the power of the computer to manage large data operations such as catalogue records was the prime driver for the existence of these organisations. In a sense, a technology enabled libraries to form these new organisations for a specific purpose while these organisations have changed their founding members and will do so again. Consortia have served their purpose well over the years but are in the process now of re-inventing themselves.

In the library landscape we now find other consortium organisations which are devoted to different purposes other than cataloguing. These might include Centre for Research Libraries (CRL), which collects research materials for their members, CAVAL, which operates a shared repository for research materials of low usage, and a growing band of similar organisations. The term consortium has now been extended to include organisations banding together for the purposes of negotiating deals for access to electronic resources. There is even an organisation of library consortia. This is International Consortium of Library Consortia (ICOLC). So the vehicle now called a consortium has found a number of purposes for librarians to achieve collective purposes.

Changing roles of and pressures on consortia

So each consortium has developed in different ways to serve its members best. These developments include staff development programmes, consultancies, low-use book and serial collaborative storage and multi-language cataloguing services. The developments have been evolutionary. Especially notable have been the emergence of joint negotiation facilities for digital products for member libraries. Excelling and leading in this area has been SOLINET,[1] based in Atlanta, Georgia. It has well over 2,500 library members and has negotiated bulk deal discounts for members seeking to subscribe to various digital services. SOLINET also negotiated a deal for all the libraries in the United States wishing to subscribe to Lexis-Nexis digital legal services. There are many consortia organisations which now exist and operate strongly in the management of digital subscription deals. Over 150 of these organisations worldwide belong to the self-managed, informal International Coalition of Library Consortia. This 'consortium of consortia' may conduct meetings dedicated to keeping participating consortia informed about new electronic information resources, and pricing practices of electronic providers and vendors.[2] So the main driver for many consortia today is to reduce the impact of their member library budgets and to discernibly add value to their member organisations. Still, the members are the dominant organisations with the consortium having its existence only as a result of the members. In a sense, they do not have lives of their own. Indeed, in the current financial crisis worldwide many smaller consortia will cease to exist or will merge with larger organisations. SOLINET, PALINET, NELINET and now BCR decided to merge. The effective date for the new organisation, Lyrasis, was 1 April 2009. They are committed to continuing their businesses as usual as the organisations are merged.[3] Each consortium organisation will reflect and cogitate on its own future. The path of SOLINET to a new future was based on its own scenario planning. The possible scenarios which were developed are included in the case studies in Chapter 9 of this book.

Clearly many of the consortia spawned by OCLC well over 40 years ago are suffering severe financial pressures as the spawning organisation itself engages in a fundamental rethink about its relationships and role in the library industry. OCLC has been engaging in 'disintermediation', having decided to sell its products and services directly to the end customer rather than through the consortia such as SOLINET, PALINET, AMIGOS and NELINET. The disintermediation is important to understand in the operating environment. From the OCLC point of view, the consortia which it spawned some years previously were no longer necessary as part of their service delivery and marketing processes. It is therefore a time to reflect on how many consortia libraries need and for what purpose. In many ways this reflects not only financial pressures for the previous parent and siblings but the changed status of OCLC with an annual turnover greater than US$50 million. OCLC, of course, has many members but its revenue streams are now not dependent on member fees. Thus the relationship to libraries is, in many ways, reversed from that of other consortia. Having said this, it is clear that membership fees have been reducing, making the fees a bond of commitment rather than a reliable income.

The future of the consortium as an organisational vehicle is strong with possibilities. It has as many futures as librarians want it to have. Kate Nevins, as the Lyrasis Chief Executive Officer, cites the benefits of consortia as being: information access and management; and people and institutional effectiveness.[4] Lyrasis now has members across 33 states in the United States and is in a strong position to shape the future landscape of library–consortia relationships. In particular, she talks about the ability of consortia to 'leverage scale and relationships with members and to combine wealth of individual relationships and partnerships'.[5]

With these developments the nature of the relationships between libraries, consortia and vendors is sharply changing. Perhaps from the perspective of the rear vision mirror we will see this time as being pivotal to how that partnership works. The traditional relationship between libraries and vendors is now extended to include consortia as real players. How this tripartite partnership works out will depend on the inventiveness and creativity of all three players. It will be testing in that two of the players are not-for-profits while the third is for-profit. The business model will be quite different and will evolve over the next few years.

What are we doing, or what is our business model?

We have talked in this chapter about the tool of the rear vision mirror. We have applied this tool to see what has happened and is happening to the Consortium as an organisation and its relationship with the 'library'. Now it is timely to understand what libraries have been doing and what they are going to do. This again can be done by using the rear vision mirror tool and then by using the disruptive technology tool (Chapter 2) to understand what could be happening and changing into the future. The business model of any organisation can be severely affected by 'disruptive technologies'. Business models are important in themselves while in our information industry they describe how each of the players in the industry add value and create a role for themselves. Business models are normally defined in terms of 'for-profit' companies. They are, however, equally pertinent to libraries except the currency is different. A company talks of revenue generated whereas the library generates value, information and service.

> A *business model* is a framework for creating economic, social, and/or other forms of value. The term *business model* is thus used for a broad range of informal and formal descriptions to represent core aspects of a business, including purpose, offerings, strategies, infrastructure, organizational structures, trading practices, and operational processes and policies. In the most basic sense, a business model is the way of doing business. It is the means by which a company can sustain itself – that is, generate revenue. The business model spells out how a company makes money by specifying where it is positioned in the value chain.[6]

Figure 3.2 Publishing business model elements

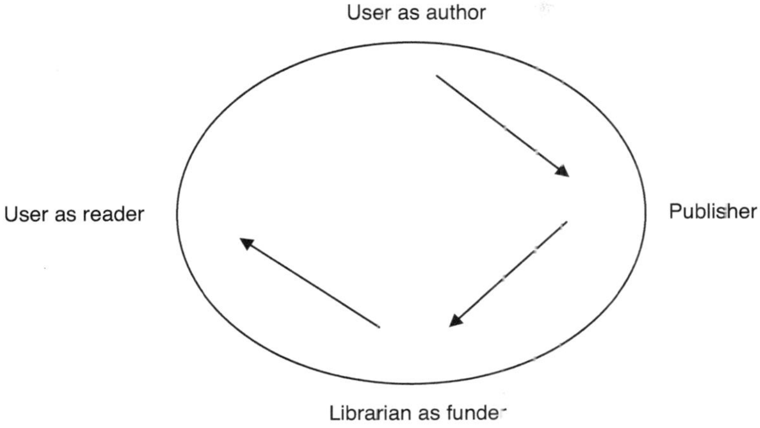

User as author

User as reader

Publisher

Librarian as funde⁻

Source: Steve O'Connor

The core business for a library, as we look through the rear vision mirror tool, has been to acquire, catalogue, store and make available published materials. This was the traditional business model for the library. Prior to the digitisation of content, the library provided the archival role by collecting, binding and storing journal and book content. The publishers saw clearly that their business model was to collect content, to publish it, and distribute it to customers – both library and individuals – in print form.

In the first model the Publisher receives the IPR from the Author and the revenue stream from the librarian. The library role in this business model is to fund the publishing enterprise and to deliver the published content to the Reader.

Now the roles have changed and with that the business models. Publishers have new business models for their operations. Publishers still have the need to generate revenue but they have different ways, or business models, for achieving that revenue. One business model is to achieve

Figure 3.3 Publishing business model flows

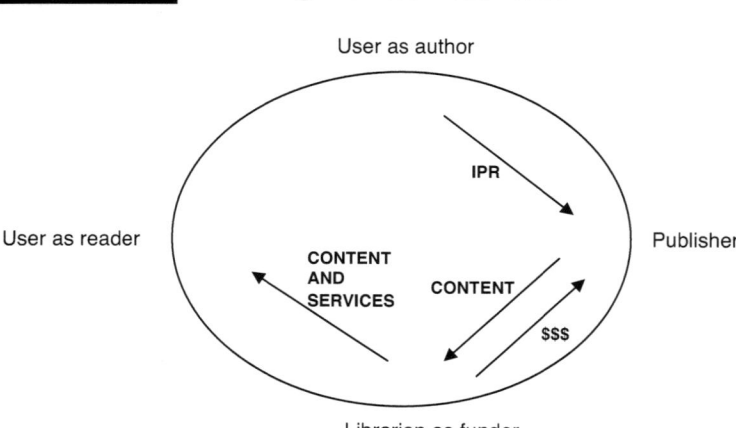

Source: Steve O'Connor

revenue by selling subscriptions to their traditional client base, the libraries. Another business model will see publishers on-selling content (which they currently own for the lifetime of the author plus seventy years) to other avenues of distribution.

A further business model will be publishers selling content or generating revenue by marketing their services and content directly to the end-user, bypassing the library. In other words, the publishers have the same traditional business model (delivering a mixture of print and digital content) but now have new business models by on-selling content, and by bypassing the library and marketing directly to the individual. In addition, they have greatly strengthened their position by securing ownership of the content through the development and enactment of copyright laws. They are still partners in the delivery of content from the author to the user but they have more options for the delivery of content and, of course, how they generate income or revenue. The diagrams show

Figure 3.4 Publishing business model alternatives

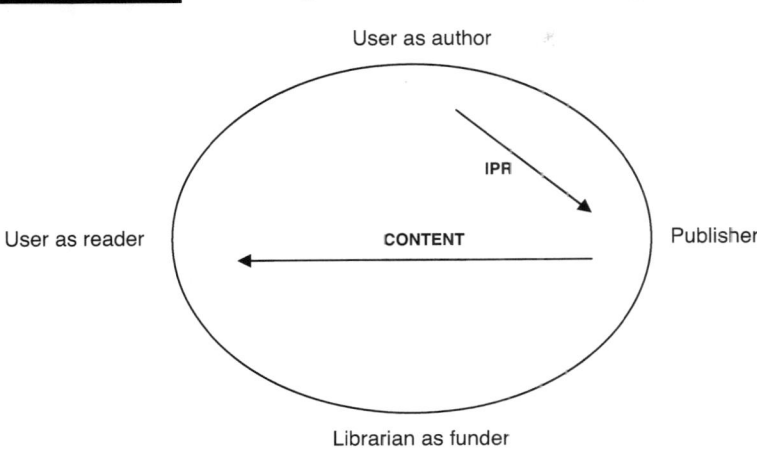

Source: Steve O'Connor

the traditional business model and also the new business models. There are other business models which are being contemplated which again do not involve the library at all.

The library, on the other hand, has a much more limited scope for its business model. It no longer collects, binds and stores journal literature. The business model for the library has been to assist or fund the publishing process (by purchasing journal and book content) and to make it available to library users. There is nothing inherently wrong with this model. The difficulty is that many of the library's users who access the digital content online do not even realise that the library has organised and funded that content to be available to them.

The Chinese use the word *Wei Jei* to describe crisis. As we have seen, however, the word has two aspects to it, *Wei* meaning danger and *Jei* meaning opportunity. The danger for libraries in having one depleted or exhausted business model is that they can be bypassed or be considered irrelevant. The opportunity is to create new business models by looking at

Figure 3.5 Publishing business model alternatives: 2

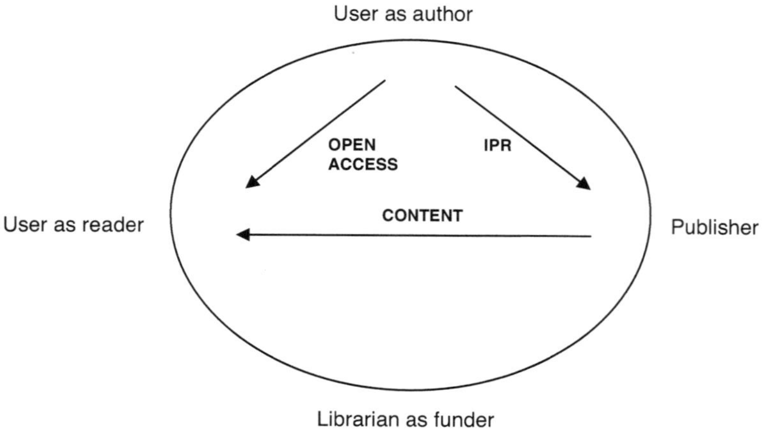

User as author

OPEN
ACCESS

IPR

CONTENT

User as reader

Publisher

Librarian as funder

Source: Steve O'Connor

new futures. In Chapter 2 there was discussion about disruptive technologies. As far as libraries are concerned the mere shift to digital delivery has been a huge disruptive technology. Digital delivery has fundamentally and inexorably changed the library's business model. Digital content or digital delivery has effectively destroyed the traditional business model. The implications of this are seen in the change in the purpose of the library building from storage to learning. The amount of space required previously for storage has now effectively halved while the user spaces have doubled at least. So what is the basic business model for the library?

Future business models

The ways in which libraries will organise themselves in the future will of course be varied. As discussed already in this chapter, the role of consortia will be incorporated into these library business relationships. Libraries will move more and more to use the services of consortia to negotiate and deliver services which they can achieve best by acting together. In many senses, this is not the rise and rise of consortia but a redefining of the roles and areas of expertise of libraries. This situation has come about because of the disruptive technologies affecting publishing and social connecting environments which were explored in Chapter 1. Libraries in the future will be an extension of consortia and consortia an extension of libraries. But they will have different roles and responsibilities.

What will be different will be the management behaviours which will be required in these altered environments. Staff who are used to hierarchical reporting relationships within a single library will find a very different environment in a wider consortia governing relationship. It will require new managerial and personal skills to achieve consensus and to execute forward actions. This is an important factor as the library staff will only be able to achieve their collective goals in this way.

Notes

1. SOLINET initially merged with PALINET to form LYRASIS. Subsequent merges included NELINET and BCR into this new enlarged consortium.
2. Available at: *www.library.yale.edu/consortia* (accessed on 8 March 2009).
3. Available at: *www.mergerupdate.org* (as consulted on 8 March 2009).
4. Nevins, K. (2010). 'Lyrasis: Great Expectations: Library collaboration in challenging times'. Academic Librarian 2. Available at: www.lib.polyu.edu.hk/ALSR2010/programme/presentation/Theme4_Nevins_Presentation.pdf (accessed on 20 June 2010).
5. Ibid.
6. Wikipedia as consulted on 14 March 2009.

4

Understanding choices

If you limit your choices only to what seems possible or reasonable, you disconnect yourself from what you truly want, and all that is left is compromise. (Robert Fritz[1])

This chapter

The chapters previous to this have dealt with the nature of scenarios, how to understand the nature of the future and the disruptive influences or forces which shape those futures. This chapter is designed to help us deal with choices arising out of those deliberations: the choices we will need to make. It will also help us understand the nature of choices and how to deal with seemingly contrasting and/or contradictory positions in those choices. This chapter will especially deal with three main techniques which start at the *simple* issue level, move through the *complex* then on to the *uncertain* event approach. These three approaches can be used together or on their own. The first is often referred to as the Axis of Uncertainty, while the second might be called Alternative Scenarios and the third is the Unexpected or Surprise Futures approach. Each of these approaches is a tool to enable us to deal with choices; choices which need to be made at some point or another.

What are choices?

We make choices every day. Life would be boring or inactive without the choices we have the opportunity to make. To make our own choices is far more important than to have them made for us. Often choices are a matter of degree. We can have a drink of wine. We can choose to drink a little or a lot. There are consequences to choices along that continuum of a little to a lot. To choose a lot of wine will have health consequences or impacts on others while we are intoxicated. Health can be described as a matter of choice. A choice can be to seek good health or not to worry about one's health. This again is a continuum. There are degrees of substance with wine also. We could choose red or white or even sparkling. This may be a matter of taste or situation but the choice is ours to make. So there are many library examples of choice. One can choose a level of service to be provided. One can choose the speed at which materials are made available in print or even electronically. One can choose to work collaboratively with other colleagues or libraries. One can choose to have more face-to-face service or more automated delivery of service.

Perhaps the first step is to understand the range of issues which are existent within an organisation. In doing this the staff can begin to understand the range of perspectives across a collective staff on the issues which matter to them. In a sense this illustrates the level of complexity and the variety of views even in one organisation. It will also illustrate the range of important issues which are not even on the radar of many in a library or information service staff.

Choices are affected by open discussion and the availability of diverse views. The Internet is often seen as an open field of views and opinions. This may be so but rather than helping to open minds and expose us to an unbiased array of unexpected viewpoints and useful information, the Internet actually causes us to become more closed minded. Cass Sunstein contends that we are witnessing an overall decline in the influence of 'General interest intermediaries,' and an increase in highly specialised areas of information, such as highly partisan cable television channels, or websites that allow us to 'personalise' the news we receive. In such a culture, he argues, 'we have the ability to see only what already interests us and to filter out any exposure to the different concerns and political opinions of fellow citizens, thus preventing a truly democratic conversation.'[2]

If an organisation is facing a period of crucial change, it is important to engage all staff in some or many parts of the planning process. This is recognising that there will be an end to this planning process and a resulting implementation phase. Alerting all members of the staff to the range of issues at the beginning of the process can only help to psychologically prepare them for the mere fact of change, whatever it turns out to be. The management of change anxiety is important from the very outset. The exercise detailed below will bring out a surprising array of issues from one staff cohort; a surprising array of issues from staff at the same employment level; a surprising array of issues which many do not even begin to recognise as being important or existent.

The prominent author G.K. Chesterton made the following observation: 'I owe my success to having listened respectfully to the very best advice, and then going away and doing the exact opposite.'[3] Chesterton was renowned for his sense of paradox and being able to highlight extremes. In this quotation, we can recognise that even the unorthodox view should be examined as a real, possible and viable choice. Exercises such as that listed above will highlight issues and concerns in the organisation's staff but will also enable some discussion of those concerns.

Exercise

This exercise is designed to involve all the staff of a library as the scenario planning process is begun.

Part 1

1. What issues do we think need to be addressed by the library considering its future? List five issues each on a separate sticky note.
2. These issues can be anything which staff from all levels of the organisation believe to be important to them or the organisation.
3. Each participant should then classify them into broad groupings along with their fellow participants. Perhaps these groupings can be categorised as Staffing, Budget, Building, Resources and so on.

Part 2

1. Talk through the issues created in each grouping.
2. Are further groupings within groupings becoming apparent? Do the participants find anything revealing or odd in the assembled thought?
3. List all the contributions and if possible determine frequencies of issues. This is important so that all staff can see their ideas being retained and will be useful as the point of departure for staff.

Linking with the work of the earlier chapters, we can now look at the range of issues confronting a library organisation but with a different perspective. If we have conducted the exercises as suggested in Chapter 2 we would have begun to understand what we think will happen to our collections over the next five to ten years. We will have views from within our organisation of its reliance on content, on print and on digital and the web. We will have explored the perceived impact which these changes will have on our budget, staff levels and skill requirements. Each of these understandings will differ from staff member to staff member; from library to library; from organisation to organisation. The important thing is that we have begun to get the organisation to look forward and to understand that the environment will be different and that, most likely, the perceived changes would happen sooner rather than later; quicker than we might anticipate. So in this process we have begun to make choices.

In understanding disruptive technologies we have looked at our library environment and have seen that technologies can emerge which radically change the business of an organisation. The emergence of the personal computer (PC) is the classic recent example. The advent of 'cloud computing' may have a similar impact. However, for libraries the emergence of the digital delivery of content to the end user has 'disrupted' the business model for libraries. It has led to the most fundamental re-examination of the library and its relationships to users, to vendors and to consortia. The environment is clearly complex and saturated with choices. If this disruption has already occurred to the library business model, then it is very important to recall this throughout the planning process.

Disruptive technologies can occur again to the library and/ or to many of the component parts of the whole industry, thus creating further impacts. For example, a narrowing of ownership of publishing houses or distributors will have an impact on the economics of the library. A population take-up of devices such as the Kindle or the iPad could have a strong impact on the nature of publishing and where publishers choose to make their content available. Publisher business models will struggle with change and the impact on their revenue streams.

Beginning to construct scenarios through choices

Axes of uncertainty

We will talk in this chapter now about simple and more complex ways of beginning to create scenarios but, as with most issues of complexity, it is best to start as simply as possible. As mentioned above, choices can often be seen to be on a continuum, from one extreme to another. Two examples are pursued below which begin to illustrate how scenarios can be constructed.

In everyday life, two choices we might confront are between degrees of financial resource and the extremes of weather. The two variables might be illustrated as per Figure 4.1.

At first glance these two sets of choices do not sit easily with each other but if they are set at cross axes, four different quadrants of potential actions emerge.

By crossing the axes each of the four quadrants can create different possibilities as illustrated by naming each quadrant as a scenario. There are four scenarios depending on the circumstances. But there are also variations should one be

Figure 4.1 Axes of uncertainty

Rich --- Poor

Hot weather ---------------------------- Cold weather

Source: Steve O'Connor

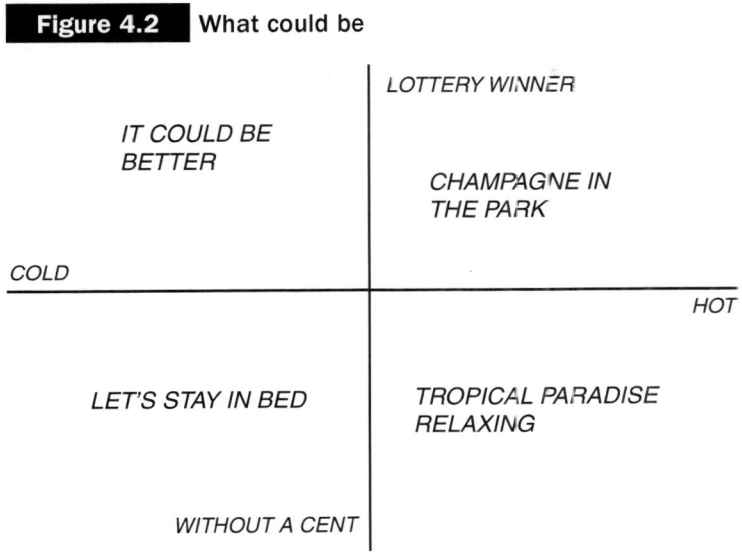

Figure 4.2 What could be

LOTTERY WINNER

IT COULD BE
BETTER

CHAMPAGNE IN
THE PARK

COLD

HOT

LET'S STAY IN BED

TROPICAL PARADISE
RELAXING

WITHOUT A CENT

Source: Steve O'Connor

positioned at different points along one or other of the axes. There are also degrees by which any scenario is emphasised depending on where the axes intersect with each other. If the vertical axis were to be moved to the left toward the cold extreme of the horizontal axis there the choices are even more stark. This is a straightforward example.

The issues identified in the earlier exercise in this chapter involving staff would provide an abundance of issues for this simple cross-axes exercise. Indeed the exercise can be and shoud be done for a variety of issues which are straining the organisation. By crossing issues which might be providing tension in the organisation, potential stories of different futures can emerge. The stories may in turn lead to the investigation of solutions or may just lead to further stories. At this stage, however, it is so important to keep minds open to different perspectives, to different outcomes, especially those which had not been entertained previously.

Figure 4.3 Axis shifting

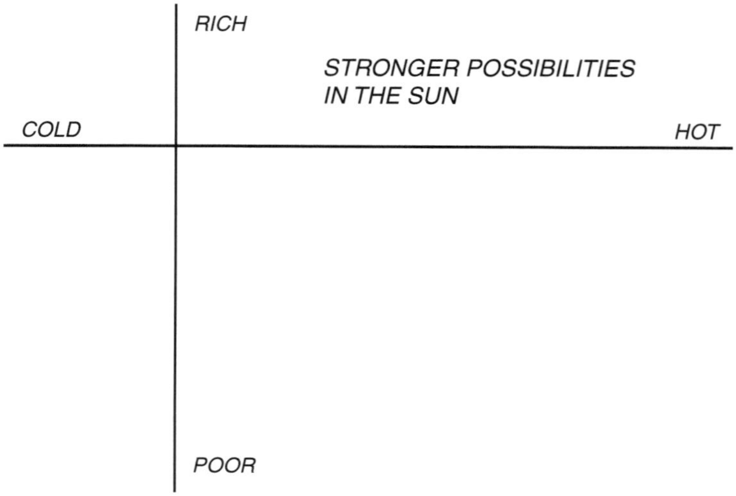

RICH

STRONGER POSSIBILITIES
IN THE SUN

COLD   HOT

POOR

Source: Steve O'Connor

A more relevant library example might be as outlined in Figure 4.3.

There are two issues here with choices to be made. Each quadrant will begin to tell a different story. From our work in Chapter 2 we began to make predictions as to where we might be on the print–digital continuum in a certain period of time. If we believe that our library will have moved very significantly toward digital delivery the library can target different positions in relation to the existing position and future chosen positions. In this way, the relevance or purposing of the physical building might be open for discussion.

The Physical Library might then develop a different purpose, a similar purpose or even a more radical one as a learning or community space. The purpose of a Library Scenario in this quadrant might be revealed through discussions around the disruptive technologies and other options within the broader organisation of which the library is part. But it begins to draw a story of where the library is

Figure 4.4   Library axes

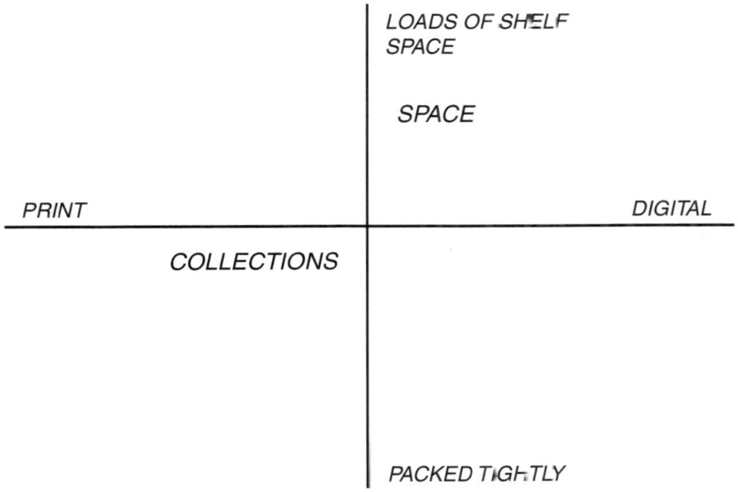

```
                              LOADS OF SHELF
                              SPACE

                              SPACE


PRINT                                              DIGITAL

              COLLECTIONS



                              PACKED TIGHTLY
```

Source: Steve O'Connor

heading. If, however, the library's research places it in the quadrant described as Digital-Tightly Packed, then the Library's story or future scenario would be quite different. This might see a strong move to digital delivery of content but a very strong legacy print collection which needs to be managed in harmony with the digital future.

Choices with timeframes in mind

To extend the scenario creation process we can introduce the element of time. In this, two critical issues for the library have emerged as outsourcing, or not, and personal service/ auto-mediation. These two issues are likely to be highly relevant in the current financial, technological and education climates. The financial environment is such that money for libraries might be tight and economies in the library operations are being sought. The outsourcing issue might be one issue while there could be a number of others. The

Figure 4.5 Libraries and learning

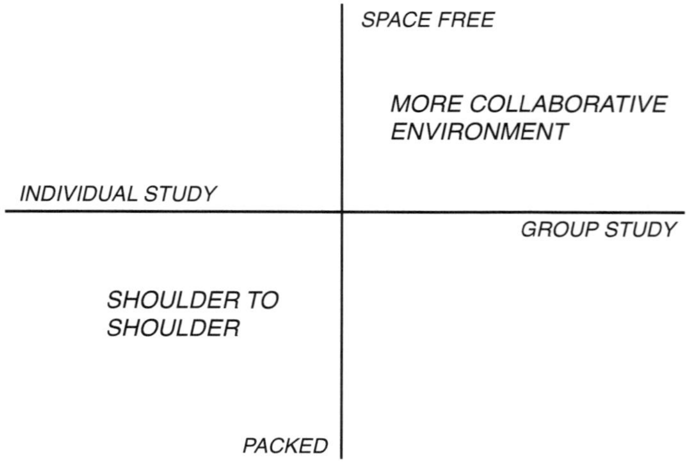

SPACE FREE

MORE COLLABORATIVE
ENVIRONMENT

INDIVIDUAL STUDY

GROUP STUDY

SHOULDER TO
SHOULDER

PACKED

Source: Steve O'Connor

concept of personal service versus auto service could be an issue arising from financial pressures but could also, as discussed in Chapter 3, be a desirable possibility as Web 3.0 technologies come more and more into play. Web 3.0 is broadly termed the 'Semantic Web', where technology will be more intuitive in interpreting user requests and retrieving relevant information. Web 3.0 offers huge potential for libraries and equally interesting threats to the future of the library service as we currently know it. So it is an issue which must be addressed. Where does your library wish to be positioned if this possibility is to happen?

In this example, the Outsourcing–Auto-mediation quadrant might be described as the Anywhere Library. In this scenario, the library might not have a physical presence but be very reliant on emerging Web 3.0 technologies, enabling the user to drive the information system themselves. Equally, one can apply time and status pointers to both of these axes which will also drive the shape of the scenario. By indicating that we are currently well away from a full

| Figure 4.6 | Library axes and time shifting |

Outsourcing

The ANYWHERE library
Complete

Auto inter-lending

None   Now   3 Years   Complete

None

Source: Steve O'Connor

auto-mediated situation and that in three years the library would still have a long way to go, two aspects are made clear. One is that the scenario approach has enabled the library to consider a future that might have otherwise been discarded or not seriously considered. It can still be allowed for in planning terms, in organisational and structural terms. Two, it gives the library a purposeful direction but with options. The library in these scenarios does not have to commit to a total outsourcing or auto-mediated approach. It is able to signal where it believes the current and future situations might be while allowing for these possibilities. A story and a vision will emerge, rather than just struggling along. A clear strategic direction and future can be seen to emerge from this technique. A way of making sense of these projections would be as shown in Figure 4.7.

As we progress this exercise it can become more and more complex in terms of the strategic issues and the stories which emanate from the quadrants. By combining the axes, the timeframe and the potential to move from one strategic state

Figure 4.7 Emerging library scenarios

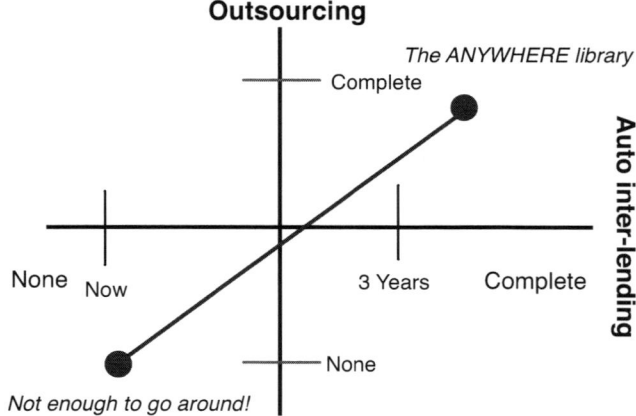

Source: Steve O'Connor

(Not enough to go around) to another (The Anywhere Library), new possibilities open up for the organisation.

This axis-with-time exercise can be used in local or departmental planning scenarios as well. The inter-lending department might want to think independently about their own positioning. The acquisitions department might wish to do something similar. The exercises of the issues, the simple and then the more complex axes work well in this local planning environment as well.

Alternative scenarios

Using this 'axis of uncertainty' technique, and a number of the issues arising from the earlier exercise, new insights can be developed. So there can be multiple axes exercises developed, only with different issues. The juxtapositioning of even previously unassociated issues can lead to interesting possibilities. The researching of the resulting 'scenarios' in the quadrants will unleash new possibilities. This is entirely natural and indeed helpful. Using these techniques and outcomes helps to reveal that, as the scenarios raise the level of the debate from issues to broader scenarios, a range of choices still exist. Organisations under pressure or in crisis often succumb to the most 'obvious' solution. A consortium organisation losing its income streams could face the obvious direction to downscale, but with intelligent scenario insights, and a little in the way of reserves, can choose to grow instead of shrink. This is a case of what Chesterton observed earlier in this chapter: go away and do the opposite. The library facing the need to change its basic business may choose to become a more relevant Resource Centre instead of maintaining its strong heritage and fundamentally changing the nature of the library business model. The most obvious is not always the most desirable. The most obvious is certainly not necessarily the most effective and sustainable for the long term.

The solutions are often wrapped in the form of paradoxes and paradoxes are contradictions.[4] Being aware of this phenomenon can begin to allow alternative solutions to be entertained and even developed. The position of paradox often blinds us, restricting our position from noticing what is possible. We can too easily reject the idea without giving it real consideration. To grow when we should be shrinking is a contradiction and we resist the adoption of this plainly absurdist position. It seems to be illogical; too illogical. To be not following the world in fashion or in practice is a contradiction and therefore difficult to entertain, let alone develop. To entertain a library without books is so against the instinct as to be extremely difficult to grasp. It is not that these contradictory positions are necessarily correct but by examining them the germ of a good scenario may be grasped and developed. So paradoxical positions can be beneficial. They allow the mind to think about things which we would not normally allow ourselves to think about. This is the kind of thinking which we want to achieve.

The excellent book *Management of the Absurd* by Richard Farson[5] delves into the issues of paradox and the absurd. Time and again he makes the point that we, as humans, think and say that we want to do something but in the end we find the possible changes deeply threatening. He talks about how relatively easy it is to develop creative ideas but shows that it is so much more difficult to accept and implement the ideas. 'The fundamental problem with creativity is that every new idea requires the manager and the work force to undergo significant change.'[6] 'Real creativity, the kind that is responsible for breakthrough changes in our society, always violates the rules.'[7] Creativity and new ideas are often negated by the fear of being different. If we are looking for breakthrough change, the earlier chapters in this book highlight that change will happen to us if we do not act; it will happen quicker than we might even rationally imagine. Change by increment or gradual change will waste the potential of an organisation to contribute and to develop. The changes need to be decisive, not immediately in action, but especially in a chosen direction.

This methodology can build on the Axes of Uncertainty as well as the tools which were developed in Chapters 2 and 3. A great deal of input can be gained from the research and insights gained through those exercises. This methodology utilises group and workshop activity to take the input and individual insights to challenge each group to develop three broad-brush scenarios which are alternative scenarios.

Imagination

Scenarios are an invention of the imagination. They are plausible stories about the possible futures for our libraries. The use of our imagination is crucial to give the stories a real and inviting flavour. The use of imagination also allows the introduction of interest and excitement to the picture being drawn of the future or the great story being written. Imagination breaks us out of the humdrum of ordinary life and into a space which is different, interesting and inviting.

Having heightened our sense of imagination we have to maintain in the stories we tell a certain level of plausibility. This does not deny us the chance to think 'outside the box'! The scenarios can and should be imaginative, plausible, stimulating and challenging. The scenarios will be about people, information and spaces (or no spaces) but they will evoke in the reader a real sense of what could be and how they may be able to identify themselves in that space or place. Not all the scenarios will be equally attractive to all the readers but this is where the debate can begin in earnest and the use of good imagination will help us get there.

Unexpected or surprise futures

This position is the logical extension of the first two approaches to scenario construction. It is the 'most unlikely' event strategy. The newspapers are littered with life-threatening events affecting the lives of us and our fellow citizens. Many or most of these events are unpredictable. They always happen to someone else. They are unexpected; they are often totally abnormal or beyond the range of our imagination or expectation. We do not go out of our homes and expect to be hit by a truck or to have the building we are living in collapse. As such we do not allow for them in our normal planning; in our normal lives. We do not allow ourselves to think of the 'unthinkable'. Therefore we do not allow for it in our planning. Planning for the attacks of 9/11 in New York was so far outside the range of possibility, it was not planned for by government officials. It was a less than 1 per cent risk situation. It was the most extreme scenario and, as such, was never taken heed of. The American Vice President was so shocked with the events of 9/11 that he turned the risk approach for American national security on its head and actually planned for the 1 or 2 per cent events. This, of course, is a hugely expensive approach but it was a decision which they felt was necessary.

Does planning for library and information service futures involve planning for the 2 per cent possibility? Perhaps. Perhaps not. But the assessment of risk is a strong reminder that there are events which are outside of what we allow ourselves to think of but are important to at least consider. Where we have talked earlier in this chapter of alternative scenarios and other variations, so it is crucial to consider an extreme scenario. It is timely also to remember that we do not have any one future; we have many. So at this stage we need to have a range of options or scenarios. The scenario which we do not allow ourselves to think of can sometimes provide direct stimulation and vital input for a more realistic final scenario.

So many writers have in recent years prophesised the death of the library or the death of the book. The book by Richard Watson, *Future Files*,[8] has presented an extinction timeline from 2000 to 2050. In this he predicts a number of things. By 2019 he predicts that libraries will be extinct. By 2020, he predicts that copyright will be extinct. By 2023, he predicts that the desktop computer will be extinct. The scenario in which all three of these predictions come true would indeed be a scenario with severe consequences for our planning.

What would we do if indeed copyright were to be abolished from the statute books? It would signal a wholesale change in the way we understand the written expression of thought or fiction. What would we do?

To entertain the extinction of libraries is much closer to home. It is absurd to our being but it has now been openly speculated about. It is talked about and even accepted as a reality soon to occur. Inevitable, say some. This is the extreme scenario. It is perhaps a very low risk as far as our thinking is concerned but it just could become a reality. What would we do?

Keeping options open

The intention of the discussion in this chapter has been to create options; to create different scenarios and to avoid leaping to a conclusion as to the best or most likely future. To leap too early is to destroy all the thinking which has been examined in the earlier chapters and the array of possibilities which are always before us. This chapter has also sought to begin the process of creating options, of naming some of these options as potential scenarios and of allowing the extremes to enter the debate and thinking.

We are now well positioned to get the best out of our people, our users, our stakeholders in the next chapter.

Notes

1. Available at: *http://thinkexist.com/quotes/robert_fritz/* (accessed on 20 July 2010).
2. O'Connor, R. (2009). 'Word of mouse: Credibility, journalism and emerging social media'. Joan Shorenstein Center on the Press, Politics and Public Policy. Available at: *www.hks. harvard.edu/presspol/publications/papers/discussion_papers/ d50_oconnor.pdf*: 10 (accessed on 20 July 2010).
3. Chesterton, G. K. (2003). Quoted In Laura Moncur's

Motivational Quotations. Available at: *www.quotationspage.com/quote/1923.html* (accessed on 20 July 2010).

4. A paradox is a statement or group of statements that leads to a contradiction or a situation that defies intuition. Paradox as defined in Wikipedia. Available at: *http://en.wikipedia.org/wiki/Paradox* (accessed on 12 February 2010).

5. Farson, R. (1996). *Management of the Absurd*. New York: Simon and Schuster.

6. Ibid.

7. Ibid.

8. Watson, R. (2008) *Future Files*. London: Nicholas Brealey Publishing.

Toward a new way of thinking

This chapter

The basic presumption or driver for this chapter is that many minds are needed to make good future decisions. It is important to think about how to achieve the involvement of as many people as possible in the future decisions for your organisation. It is difficult to achieve this involvement but it is more difficult to get people to think for themselves and to articulate those views. To gain real options and a diverse set of views, it is crucial to get views from all different perspectives and to allow for the different ways in which people think and perceive the world around them. This chapter is devoted to achieving the best involvement and the best articulation of views across the organisation and its user communities.

How to organise for decisions

Cass Sunstein[1] has written widely about how we seek to make decisions through the processes of deliberation. In any group deliberation situation it is important to avoid 'same thinking' or 'groupthink'. This is where ideas do not get tested in a genuine fashion because conformity to a certain way of thinking is deemed to be the appropriate way to present the findings. Because the group is understood to think in a particular fashion, 'outside' ideas are not easily allowed in. Irving Janis is acknowledged as suggesting that 'groups may well promote unthinking uniformity and dangerous self-censorship, thus failing to combine information and enlarge the range of arguments'.[2] The point of this scenario planning process is to extract from the members of the group the maximum value of the individual and collective insights. A failure to achieve a maximum understanding of the environment in which the library is and plans to be would be dangerous and would blunt the value of any planning processes. Sunstein highlights that the failure of the CIA to report correctly on the Weapons of Mass Destruction in Iraq was partly due to 'groupthink' and not being able to obtain and use information which its staff actually possessed. He also describes another investigation into the disaster of the Columbia space shuttle crash where similar stultifying processes occurred, again even though many of employees had the correct information and knowledge. Individually, they could not think or see anything different to what the group 'allowed' them to think. The group subconsciously had placed boundaries on what was allowable and what was not.

In any scenario planning process it is crucial that the information gathering allows time and periods of introspection. The information gathering should also be a group process. By working as a team, that group of persons can establish a rapport with each other and with the information gathered. By allowing time for the process the team has more time to get to know and understand each other and also to grow the inter-connectiveness of their observations. Information gathered in one quarter will make a connection with that from another quarter. Strange connections will begin to emerge and a group understanding of the various sources of relevant information will also potentially throw up 'left-field' information.

A good example of this is *The Charleston Report: Business Insights into the Library World*.[3] This very short publication provides brief collections of information, data and insights from many sources. The insights resulting from this eclectic collection lead to further and unexpected views for the future of individual libraries. Another source is *Access: Asia's newspaper on electronic services and products*.[4] This small newspaper does have a connection to the iGroup, a large distributor of information services and products across Asia, but the editor, Clive Wing, manages to capture the current and topical issues in articles that are easy to read and digest. Research is so important to opening eyes to different points of view.

Another way of seeing the value of divergent views is to understand the work on intelligences by Howard Gardner. In distinguishing intelligence capabilities our perception of 'brightness' quickly changes. Gardner wrote and researched extensively on issues surrounding our understanding of intelligence, creativity and leadership. He trained in social and educational psychology. His studies pursued the breakthroughs by individuals which led to genuine change and creativity. *The Theory of Multiple Intelligences* was first published in 1983. In this work, he defines the seven types of intelligence capabilities as:

1. *Linguistic:* the sort shown, in the extreme, by poets. It is also the capability to write and express ideas. The ability to work in a multi-lingual environment.

2. *Logical/Mathematical:* not only displayed in logic and mathematics but in science and business generally. Society values those who can balance budgets and indeed make money.

3. *Spatial:* the ability to hold in your head a model of the organisation of the world around you. It is also the

ability to work in a space in three dimensions. When we talk of the 'library without walls', perhaps we need a different spatial sense. Typically this could be the skills of an architect or an artist.

4. *Musical:* This is self-explanatory. It is another intelligence of balance and rhythm.

5. *Bodily/Kinesthetic:* the sort shown by, say, dancers or sports people; the use of the whole or parts of the body to fashion some product or performance.

6. *Interpersonal:* the awareness of how to get along with others. This is also the capability to 'encourage' others to work together and to work to an agenda. This is a key attribute of the leader. In a world where change is also a constant, this is a vital leadership intelligence.

7. *Intrapersonal:* self-knowledge. This enables us to move beyond self-doubt. It reflects knowledge or confidence to trust one's own judgement or set of work or life experiences; rather than continuing to consult or avoid taking a decision.[5]

As the Australian Alistair Mant indicates in his book *Intelligent Leadership*: 'The effect of [existing educational systems is] to over-educate and over-promote *narrow* people – those who are especially practised in (for example) the logical/mathematical and linguistic capabilities while neglecting the *complementary* capabilities of other potentially valuable people.'[6] In our context here in this book we are seeking to recognise that we do not think 'outside the box' as often as we ought. Systems are created in which we comfortably reside and operate. It is only when we are set the task of moving differently that we struggle to think of different ways of doing what has been very familiar. If we were set the task of re-inventing the library, would we be able to do so? Mant draws on the work of Gardner to find a way of explaining how breakthroughs can occur in different fields of endeavour which can fundamentally change the way in which the activity or the field are perceived or how they operate. Equally, we can view the intelligences or perspectives which many people can offer on future directions for a library. He, like Gardner, draws from the lives of people he has researched the approaches to their life's work which illustrate the strengths of different types of intelligence. It is reassuring that the most successful people in terms of leadership or changing perceptions of industries do not have a standard set of qualifications. They often think differently; they see things which others can only imagine. Albert Einstein once said: 'I am enough of an artist to draw freely on my imagination. Imagination is more important than knowledge. Knowledge is limited. Imagination encircles the world.'[7] So different perspectives and 'heretical' thinking will introduce new concepts, ideas and perspectives into a group.

As Mant says: 'Judgement is what you do when you don't (and can't) know what to do.'[8] The true essence of leadership is to change and shift systems. Leadership in this sense is to see the world differently and to be able to influence others to work with the leader to adopt the change into normal operations. To do this is to recognise how the future library model should be shaped to meet the information need of its community. There is a need to fundamentally understand the business models which libraries currently operate in. The business model defines the range of services the library intends to present to a clientele whose needs they understand. It also defines the way in which libraries operate with each other and the publishing or, more broadly, the information industry. An apposite example of this is the traditional business model which publishers have had in the subscription model. Here the financial costs of publishing have been borne by subscriptions through libraries. The more subscriptions the greater the revenue the greater the profit. Essentially the business model is to enable the communication of peer-reviewed information from the author to the reader. The publisher provides the means while the library provides the funds.[9] So leadership and thinking differently have much in common.

Exercise

This exercise is designed to stimulate imagination and creative thinking.

Part 1

1. What if we were to consider new models of publishing and the place of the library in them?
2. The existing model of publishing is reflected in the circle.
3. Each participant should understand where the dollars are in this model along with their fellow participants.

Part 2

1. Talk through the issues raised by the existing model.
2. Break into small groups and design new models.
3. Re-form into one group and determine how many models have been created. Are there any genuinely different models?

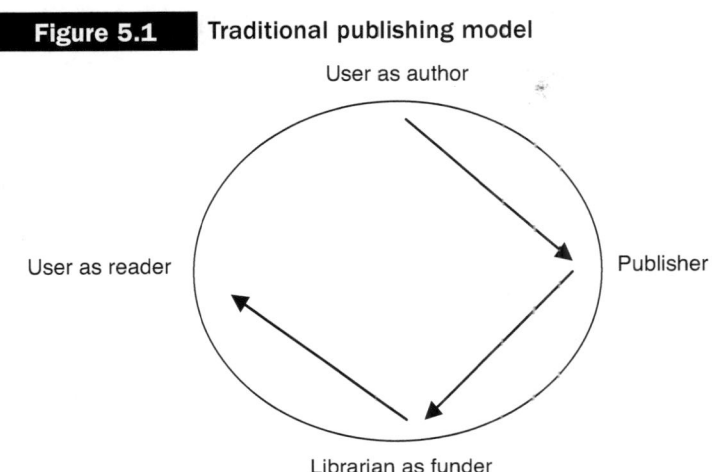

Figure 5.1 Traditional publishing model

User as author

User as reader

Publisher

Librarian as funder

Source: Steve O'Connor

Is it all straightforward?

The principal reason for any scenario planning is to best position the library for the future. The future should be one at least three to five years hence. We have already seen in earlier chapters that the rate of societal and technological change is vast indeed. The Rear Vision Mirror exercise has demonstrated how fast change is. It is only in this timeframe that we can expect to gain the best positioning. It is only in this timeframe that we can expect to give effect to the changes which come out of this process. But it must be recognised that there will be change through this process. Much can and will be achieved in this timeframe. Change is the only constant! It is difficult for staff at all levels in the organisation to deal with the change which will come through the ideas and directions which arise and are agreed to as the Preferred Scenario. It is untrue to say that the change will affect those at the lower end of the library hierarchy more than at the upper levels. The extent of the impact will depend on the attitude of individuals, the length of service in particular positions, their career position and their career or life aspirations. So the management of change will be a major component of the scenario planning process as well as its outcomes. Achieving engagement in the planning is so important for the implementation phase. So at this stage of working through to new scenarios it is very useful to understand the classic positions which organisations go through in dealing with where they are now and where they might wish to be.

The classic organisation steps through which an organisation goes consist of these four phases as it come to grips with change.

Each of these steps requires understanding and planning to deal with detachment of staff and to allow them as full a participation as possible. Typically, organisations have many of their staff in employment for long periods of time. Many of these organisations have the average age of their staffs to be close on 60 years of age and the prospect of change is not very inviting. 'After all it has worked very well up until this,

Figure 5.2 Classic change cycle

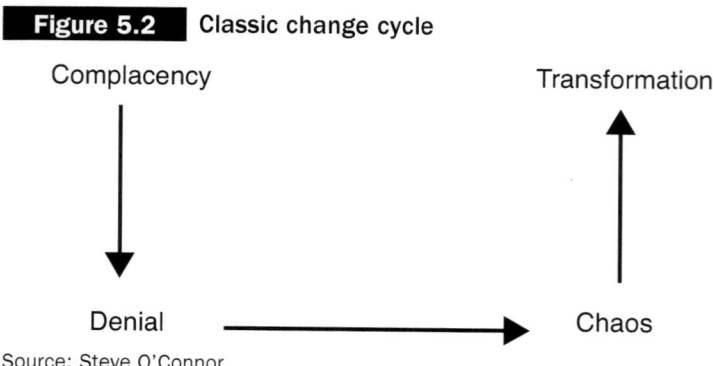

Source: Steve O'Connor

thank you very much.' Many staff have also been in their existing positions for many years and are either very happy and content where they are or may be actually looking for more stimulation and scope to act. Still, the organisation often looks the same as it has for many years. This is one piece of evidence that the organisation is *complacent*. Another may be the extent to which the organisation moves outside its own walls, often and candidly, into its user and governing communities to listen to what is being said. Having begun the process of scenario planning, staff in the organisation could be seen to be in a state of *denial*. Denial might describe that they do not believe that anything has to change; 'It will all move easily and nicely without too much interference.' It is highly desirable to engage all the library staff in the planning and contribution phases so that their ideas, positive or negative, can come to the fore and be included in the information-gathering and research phases.

What happens typically to any organisation which has moved through these first two phases is that there is what could be described as *chaos*. This is a state where the familiar structures are being threatened or potentially changed, sometimes significantly. The place which individuals had for themselves in their work world has been challenged. The desk is no longer the area of familiarity and security. Procrastination can take many forms in this circumstance. Research indicates that people can be unrealistically optimistic about their capacity to undertake change.[10] The further ahead the change, the more procrastination occurs. If the present is not so uncomfortable as to force change then it will be postponed. Getting engagement rather than resistance is the most critical issue in selecting different futures for the organisation. It is easier to sit out the process and snipe on the side. This option is to be avoided.

It is worth noting, given that change is inevitable and actually happening, that staff who have been in positions for a long period of time will strongly opt for different positions with differing responsibilities in this phase of change. This is especially if they have been engaged with the process from Day One. Staff involvement might not have been intensive but if they have been able to hear of the reasons for this new planning, they may have actually become interested in what might happen. The exclusion of staff at any level across the organisation can only create disharmony and conflict at this penultimate stage of the change process. Not all staff will benefit from involvement; not all staff will want to be involved other than tangentially; the levels of participation and knowledge can always be achieved across the organisation to allow for these different levels of interest. The final phase is obviously that of *transformation*. This is not reached easily or quickly. It may not be realised for a longish period of time. The organisation which has a Preferred Scenario to pursue will start to smoothly create the *transformed* organisation. We might all have differing ideas of when the transformed organisation is actually achieved. In a later chapter, there will be a discussion regarding the management of the 'end game'. From another perspective, if plans are being put in place and executed toward that Preferred Scenario, then, it could be argued, the transformation has already occurred. Transformation is how the organisation views itself; the energy it has and the sense of purpose and drive.

So it is wise to be aware, to be prepared for the different phases of change which will occur. The preparation will be all the stronger and effective for a wide, if not total, involvement of the staff and clientele from the beginning and through the whole process. Politically, the more ownership there is by staff and the clientele, including the users and governance, the stronger the longer-term commitment there will be toward the achievement of the Preferred Scenario.

Confronting sameness

In constructing scenarios it is important to construct genuinely different and perhaps radically different models. It is important to have the mind free if real openness or creativity is to occur. This is not easy. The commonly quoted opinion of Thomas Edison – 'Genius is one percent inspiration and ninety-nine percent perspiration'[11] – is entirely apposite. As Gardner analyses our intelligences above: intelligence comes in all forms; so it is that good ideas come in all shapes and sizes. It is a matter of allowing them through the filters of group thinking; of allowing different perspectives to emerge and to be heard. One perspective on this issue is that the best ideas are not new ideas but rather new perspectives or combinations of ideas. Andrew Haragdon relates the

Figure 5.3 Same thinking

story of Thomas Edison's invention of the light bulb.[12] Edison's first application for a patent was rejected because his invention infringed the patent rights of another inventor. 'Edison's contribution was not inventing electric light, but in combining it with improvements in generators, wiring, materials and business models.'[13] So it could be with libraries. It is mostly defined that libraries are in the business of collecting, storing and disseminating information as books and journals.

Another perspective might be that libraries are really in the business of publishing but have increasingly outsourced that activity to commercial publishers. Looking at the expenditure levels of libraries across the world to publishers, it is an extraordinary amount of money each year. It would be measured in the hundreds of billions of dollars. It was true to note that superannuation funds flock to investments in publishing companies because of the high amounts of cash flowing through their accounts, the very low rates of bad debt and the consistent growth year upon year. The Open Access debate discussed in Chapter 2 is a good example of a new approach to an old problem. This is where the desire to have research available and peer reviewed is achieved via a different business model. But even within this 'new solution' there are many different models: where the library pays for the publication, where the author pays or where publicly funded research is subsidised for wide and free dissemination. There are many solutions buried in each solution. But many existing solutions are tomorrow's burdens. This is especially the case when an idea can be so entrenched in the industry that an alternative is almost impossible to think of. In this situation the 'same thinking' approach blinds the whole industry to new or alternative solutions. The presence of different stakeholders in the planning session changes the dynamic and enables more open thinking. Unless there is open thinking, disruptive technologies can so easily and readily slip beneath the radar and not even be considered. This has been discussed in Chapter 2. The invention of the Personal Computer slipped beneath the collective thinking of large mainframe computer companies who had their futures firmly fixed on mainframe computing. They were so firmly fixed in their thinking that they could not begin to entertain how a small, underpowered but mobile personal computer could possibly replace their business model. But it did.

Exercise

This exercise is designed to help you think differently or to confront rigid thinking.

Part 1

1. What if we were to list tools that we consider essential now in our home or work lives? By reflecting on an established conception of a tool, its origin and purpose, we can come to understand the dangers in complacency.

Part 2

1. Each member of the group is to list five tools which they consider essential to their daily work or home lives.
2. Select one 'home' and one work tool from the collective input.
3. Brainstorm firstly how these tools came into existence and for what purpose.
4. Brainstorm how there could be future alternatives allowing radically different elements to surface.

The MARC record has been essential to modern library operations. It has been used to provide order to library records, allowing libraries globally to exchange information about particular materials or published items.[14] The MARC record came into existence only with the emergence of the computer as a means to store descriptive data for library materials and to be able to share that data. A consequence of this development was that the humble MARC record was a 'disruptive technology' to the highly reputable profession of cataloguing. Cataloguing was previously seen to be the core skill of the profession. It was seen as the basis for the future of the library. It was the core subject which every student of librarianship had to study ... and pass. Now, the modern cataloguing department either does not exist or is a vastly scaled down version of its predecessor. The disruptive technology to the MARC record could now be seen to be free text search or what might be more universally called the 'Google search'. Yet are libraries and their record structures ready for this development? Already Google Book and Google Scholar can retrieve virtually any book which exists somewhere in a library. But, as a profession, we work earnestly to maintain the MARC structure and only reluctantly allow the user to search the way they wish to.

One of the identified issues which can lead to a 'blindness' to strategically important issues is the size of the organisation. The larger the organisation the more difficult it is to get the different streams of the organisation to talk or to reflect on the performance and potential of other streams to that organisation. Yet it is crucial that these ideas or commitment to one viewpoint in an organisation interact with the viewpoints elsewhere in that organisation in a healthy and constructive manner. Nothing is sacred if scenario planning is to be effective! This is clearly not to say that all existing structures, tools or services are redundant or ineffective. It does, however, mean that they all should be tested using the various tools and exercises which this book has explored.

Research as a group

As part of the process of constructing the scenarios it is important to gather as much information as possible about the library, its performance, its usage, its reception in the communities which it serves and in the professional networks in which it operates. It is also important to gather demographic data about the state of publishing for the types of materials collected by the library, the publishing rates of books and journal titles, their costs over a period of years, the financial support given by the institution, and the numbers of staff and their levels of employment. It is important to document trends in all these areas. To benchmark one's own library with peers, locally and nationally and even internationally, is then feasible. Another research group should be surveying the literature to pick up on the major trends affecting one's own library sector and libraries generally. In this, some of the best insight will be found outside of the library literature. The assignment of the group appointed to gather information for the scenario planning process is to present their findings as trend data and with other insights into the library's present and future positions. Data should be presented in as simplified a manner as feasible. Graphical representation of the data is often useful for better understanding. If the environmental understanding is presented in different sections, it would be useful to have a half a dozen bullet-point observations at the end of each section and an overall Executive Summary of the more important observations, again in bullet points. Being concise, thinking in big pictures and being honest in the representation of the data is to be effective. One's own interpretation of the data should not be strongly represented at this stage of the process. An honest portrayal of the overall picture from as many aspects as possible will guarantee more committed involvement by all participants in the process later.

Collecting information about the environment in which your organisation is operating is critical, but it is crucial that it be open and wide-ranging. Reading Schwartz on this topic is instructive. He spends a whole chapter on this: 'Information-hunting and gathering'. He describes the process:

> The scenario process thus involves research – skilled hunting and gathering of information. This is practiced both narrowly – to pursue facts needed for a specific scenario – and broadly – to educate yourself, so that you will be able to pose more significant questions. Investigation is not just a useful tool for gathering facts. It hones your ability to perceive. Even your specific purpose in any particular research project is tagged to your inbred assumptions. You seed out those facts and perceptions which challenge those assumptions. You look for *dis*confirming evidence.[15]

In gathering your research and evidence remember to be honest and open in what is found and reported. The excellent book by David Hawkins on project strategy based on the classic Chinese book *The Art of War* reveals the importance of risk:

> The biggest risk for most business ventures, however, is to adopt a risk-averse culture, which will stifle valuable opportunities and create a major risk of rigidity. Even

worse, this approach will stop innovation and the lateral thinking attitude that is necessary to build or try alternative ideas.[16]

This is the time in the process to ensure that everything is open, that all possibilities are possible.

Notes

1. Sunstein, C. (2006). *Infotopia*. Oxford: Oxford University Press, p. 11.
2. Ibid., p. 12.
3. The Charleston Report: *Business insights into the library world*. Published bi-monthly by the Charleston Company. ISSN 1091-1863.
4. Available at: *www.aardvarknet.info/access/number44/month news.cfm?monthnews=01* (accessed 20 July 2010).
5. Mant, A. (1999). *Intelligent Leadership*. Sydney: Allen & Unwin, p. 41.
6. Ibid., p. 40.
7. O'Connor, S. (2006). 'The heretical library manager: The library manager for the future' *Library Management* 27(1/2): 62–71.
8. Mant, op. cit., p. 48.
9. O'Connor, op. cit.
10. *The Economist*, 2 January 2010, p. 55.
11. Available at: *www.bartleby.com/59/23/edisonthomas.html* (accessed on 12 April, 2009).
12. Hargadon, A. (2008). 'Creativity that works', in Jing Zhou and Christina Shalley (eds), *Handbook of Organizational Creativity*. New York: Lawrence Erlbaum Associates, p. 324.
13. Ibid.
14. The collapse of UKMARC and AUSMARC into one MARC record format highlighted the need to achieve better economics. This reality will also confront CHINA MARC which at this stage is incompatible with the MARC records. The gradual

disappearance of the national MARC format highlights not only the economic but also the global nature of the information or library business.

15. Schwartz, P. (1991). The Art of The Long View. New York: Doubleday Currency, p. 64.

16. Hawkins, D. E. and Rajagopal, S. (2008). *Sun Tzu and the Project Battle Ground*. New York: Palgrave Macmillan, p. 53.

6

Designing your process

This chapter

The purpose of this chapter is to enable the reader to consider the very practical processes by which the scenarios can be created. The earlier chapters have effectively 'set the scene' and will be drawn upon to illustrate the process being described in the following pages. The process is a suggested one and is not the only way to achieve the scenarios. The exercises illustrated in the earlier chapters are especially useful in achieving input to the steps in this process.

> The illiterate of the twenty-first century will not be those who cannot read and write, but those who cannot learn, unlearn and relearn. (Alvin Toffler)[1]

Not every process is the same

The case studies in Chapter 9 provide examples of what various organisations have achieved in Scenario Planning.[2] Each organisation is different; each is in a different country; each is in a different library sector; one is not even a library but a library consortium organisation. So diversity is highlighted in the case studies. In the same way, the processes by which the scenarios were reached and managed is different, shaped by circumstance, by political realities; by the communities which are served and by the history and position of the organisation itself.

Scenario construction beginnings

The process described in this book will lead to a Preferred Scenario for your organisation. The process should be modified where it is deemed necessary. But if an organisation decides to embark on this process, it should fully commit to the process and be bold. Within your organisation there will be issues. Some of these issues will include a fear of a 'loss of control' in the process. Some of your colleagues may wish to 'tone the process down', or to use a more controlled process of simple strategic planning. These issues are a measure of the risk which your organisation may wish to entertain in designing the process. It may be a measure of a fear of the unknown and a fear of losing control in a process which seeks very strong involvement of the organisation's stakeholders as well as the uncertain nature of what they may contribute through this process. It is a genuine concern for the owners of the process. It is important to have clear and open discussions at the senior levels of your organisation as to the nature of the process, the likely outcomes, the possible roadblocks and the organisation's taste for risk. Having said all of this, the level of risk in losing control of the process is not high. This book contends that it is a greater risk not to engage in an open and frank discussion on the future position for the library and information service – a far greater risk!

When your organisation considers a scenario planning process, it is inherently recognising that the methods used in the past have not drawn out all the issues relating to where the organisation ought to be or be heading. The scenario planning process will not predict the future. It will not allocate the organisation's resources to this activity or project. It will not establish new courses overnight. It will, however, construct stories of what might be! It will enable the organisation, its stakeholders, and staff to be excited about what might be and to embrace that future which might be seen to be three or five years into the future. The scenario planning process will construct a word story of your organisation's agreed preferred future which will draw all the players together in one 'vision' of what should be. The shape of a library's future is not or should not be driven only by the library managers but by all the members of its community. The professional library staff of course drive the process and provide the professional input. In this way there is far less risk that the future will not be owned by all, and that it will not be relevant to the organisation's users. The imagination should dominate the scenario process; do not be dragged back by an overwhelming sense of reality past and present.

The suggested process

This book can now summarise the process of scenario construction as having seven steps. Each of these steps draws on the earlier chapters of this book and the exercises contained in them.

1. Design of the actual process

As discussed above, this step requires a commitment to see the process through. It also describes who will be engaged in the process and the extent of stakeholder engagement in the process. There are two basic audiences that will need to be part of the process, each for different reasons. Firstly, each library organisation or information service will have a community of stakeholders. Secondly, there will be a vital and very interested community of staff who could be very affected by the decisions in this process.

If your community base is large, there will be an issue of how participants will be invited to partake in the process.[3] Is it to engage various representative student bodies at the undergraduate and postgraduate levels? Is it to engage key senior academic leaders in the community? Should this be at the Dean level or Head of Department? Should the Vice-President or equivalent level or the Mayor be invited to participate? Is it to engage various community organisations? In a consortium organisation, is it to engage Board members and all or some of the library members? The best path always is to involve a representative group of senior stakeholders who will be able to lend their weight to the process and its outcomes. These people will become champions for the Preferred Scenario at the end of the process. They will speak to the process and for the outcomes in many more fora than the library staff will be privileged to attend.

It is also very important to recognise another demographic. The Agreed Preferred Scenario will be focused on serving the organisation's primary clientele so they should also be strongly involved in the process. In the case of an academic library, a future planning horizon for a time three or five years into the future will inevitably be for a student cohort which is not yet enrolled at the university. It is crucial to remember that the organisation being prepared for is for a generation which is sharply younger than the planners of this process. The generation will also be younger than the student cohort who will actually participate in the process! This will apply for most library sectors. Age will shape perceptions and outlooks. So it will be important to have as wide a representation as possible of the age groupings in your stakeholders.

These are questions concerning the composition of stakeholders in the process. The actual numbers of members of your community who are engaged in the process will depend largely on your choice and decision.

2. Understanding the community and environment

Understanding the broader environment as well as the local impacts is imperative in commencing this process. Articulating these impacts in various documents for the consideration of the Scenario Construction Group will provide their foundation for understanding. The analysis of the forces at play in the library and in its wider environment will greatly help. Understanding, for instance, the rate of activity in the library in terms of acquisitions, print versus electronic, and use activity in the physical and virtual libraries, as well as trends, is very useful. Analysing the trends in publishing in print and electronic and in the subject areas of interest to your community will provide an understanding of the extent to which the community is served with quality and relevant content. Projecting models for the possible development of and access to the Internet would enable some projected understanding of what impact these developments could have on library models. Understanding the future and trend funding impacts on the parent organisation is also useful. The organisation may be growing, may be under pressure, may be under review or may not see the relevance of the library. These and other analyses help create a broad understanding of the past, existing and future environments. They can be presented as documents to those who will participate in the focus groups and the Scenario Construction Workshop to inform them. Much of this is discussed in the next chapter.

Conducting Focus Groups to ascertain the issues from the community will also form a significant input into the process. The issues arising from both processes can be juxtaposed using the axes methodology described in Chapter 4. A number of these axes exercises will enable the various forces at play in the environment of the future to be contrasted.

3. Getting your chosen community to work together

The moment of truth is now arriving as all the preparation has been done. All the briefing documents for the groups have been chosen. We are now moving into the final phases where these groups contribute to the actual construction of the scenarios. It is a narrowing of the range of people who are involved and a heightening of the sense of destiny with the created scenarios.

Focus groups

There will be two types of focus group. They will be User and Staff focus groups. They will be separately conducted and provide different but valuable input. The output will reflect the general self-interest of that group. This output from each focus group should be recorded for later use. Differences in the range and intensity of the issues from each group will reflect the interest and perspectives of that demographic group. Issues from student groups will reflect issues peculiar to the interests and understanding of that group. They will importantly reflect the ways in which that generation wish to study and the facilities which they would prefer to have in order to achieve that environment. If one of the exercises carried out with this group was to list their five top issues for the future library, then the results will be a rich field to examine. A general grouping of the results will reveal much. By this, I mean to roughly create categories into which the issues may fall. The categories may be Building, Learning, Technology, Finance and so on. The number of issues in each of these categories will diminish. A word count is a more sophisticated view of the interests of each group. This can be aggregated and cross-sliced to understand the different demographic interests.

The staff groups will often display different perspectives about the future than the students, for instance. There will be elements here of insecurity as the environment which they have known and been comfortable in is now being made subject to change.

Scenario construction workshop

This workshop is the vehicle by which the scenario will be constructed. It is therefore important to have its composition well thought through. This workshop will provide all the data and orientation for the possible futures of your organisation. You have already defined the groups who are your organisation's stakeholders, in terms of use, funding, partnership (internal and external), staff and suppliers. It is important to invite a range of these stakeholders to participate in the workshop. It is important to be careful to achieve a balance of senior and more junior people to create a wide cross-section of interests for the workshop. It is also good to identify some members of the community who will naturally act as protagonists; who will add controversial or more 'radical' views; who will think 'outside of the box'. An effective workshop will have between 30 and 40 attendees.

The facilitator for the workshop must have a fluent understanding of the ambition and desired outcome of the workshop. That person should be familiar with scenario planning techniques and the need to use imagination and to create stories about the organisation's future without trying to bed the stories down in a strategic plan. The facilitator should allow the stories to develop almost organically and without rush or pushing in a particular direction or other. All the good ideas need to come out of the workshop participants as naturally and easily as is possible.

4. Suggested ways to operate the scenario construction workshop

The group who eventually form this workshop will never have worked together before. Many will not know each other at all, or perhaps only by reference. The environment of the workshop facility needs to be casual, with good food easily available. It is desirable to form the groups beforehand so that different interests and attitudes are contained as much as possible in each group. In a total workshop of 40 persons, five groups of eight persons might be formed. Each group should ideally have a senior library person to explain any issues which the group might have about the process or certain details which they might want clarified. The staff person can also reinforce that the group does have the power to suggest change and different outcomes! An 'ice breaker' exercise is useful to make people feel relaxed and help them get to know each other. A discussion about the environment is again useful to set the scene for these participants, as also would be a summary (with the full focus group data available when requested) of the focus groups and their views and desired directions. Drawing these issues into a group-wide discussion is useful to bring out the different and sometimes diverse perspectives. Every outlandish idea, every different perspective, every half-thought needs to be encouraged. All these ideas begin to create a stimulating atmosphere of possibilities and indeed probabilities. The groups will be encouraged to work together, teasing out this idea or that, this experience or that, this long-held view or that, and especially perspectives of what students and teachers or community leaders need from their future library. The final outcome will not be one idea or another but an amalgam of all of these perspectives.

5. Draw up the scenarios

At this stage there should be a further discussion about scenarios; examples of other institutional outcomes, such as those in the case studies in Chapter 9, will give the participants a flavour of what is being aimed for. It is not the objective of the workshop to finalise the polished words of each proposed scenario but to provide the skeleton and the major characteristics. It is a good exercise for each group to look at the issues which they or others have raised and start to lay down what they see as the most important or the most contentious. They can use the exercise of the axes to start imagining stories of what might be in the different quadrants.

The task of each group is to create three scenarios. The scenarios might represent three different levels of risk or a range of possibilities such as the present, an intermediate future, and a more radical future. The creation of three futures ensures that a range of options and choices remains in play as long as possible. It also avoids the debate, at this time, as to which future is best. Participants and the wider community will be attracted to each scenario but not all to the one scenario. The creation of three scenarios also enables these stories to be taken back to the community as evidence of possibilities which could be chosen for their organisation.

In creating a scenario a strong and evocative title for each scenario is good to identify their core elements. You can note some of the titles used in the case studies. The dynamics of the groups in the scenario construction process will always create something clear and defining about each scenario. What is the nature of the scenario being drawn up? Is it memorable? Does it capture the essence of the words being used to describe the scenario?

In creating a scenario it is important also to allow for change. The chart below looks at the range of possibilities which can exist. The options can be to stay within existing operating conditions or to change realities. This is often a useful scenario because it is a natural extension of the present and, in this way, is easy to create and imagine. It is within 'the existing paradigm' or mode of operating but it is a viable future. If the community wishes to accelerate change but without doing anything too radical then this may be the kind of outcome which is achieved or is described as a scenario.

The 'Futures Trap' is an imaginative option and allows for popular conceptions of where future technologies are taking us. It can stretch our own horizon and allow all those ideas which we may not have wanted to entertain or been able to

Figure 6.1 Paradigm targets

Source: Steve O'Connor

afford. It may be the library which is very high tech providing unimaginable services or a scenario where the 'library' does not even exist. This scenario allows the futurist in each of us to come to the fore. We can allow our imaginations to run riot; we all have that imagination. This is often a release scenario. But it will have many serious and operational issues which will be kept in view with this scenario.

The 'Mindless Action' effectively is to do nothing. It may be to shuffle the old strategic plan and spruce it up a little but it is not going to fundamentally change the way in which the organisation is seen by its community and staff.

The workshop participants should be asked to create three scenarios, to describe each by providing a list of, say, ten bullet points outlining the various aspects to each scenario and to give each scenario an appropriate and lively title.

While working in a workshop with a number of groups, with each producing three scenarios, it is exciting to hear their presentations and to look at the degree of overlap between the creative efforts by the participants. The process of having the workshop merge different scenarios can mostly collapse twenty-four or so scenarios (assuming that there are eight groups and each group produces three scenarios) into three or maybe four scenarios. Once this is done, then the work of the workshop has been completed. The workshop objective is to achieve this collective view.

6. *Writing up the scenario*

This is a creative and stylistic effort by a writer engaged in this process or at least a close observer of it. The writer needs a sharp understanding of what is being said by the participants, as well as an understanding of issues and language in the library and information profession and also in the wider educational or community environment. The style of each writer will vary and cannot be prescribed. It is crucial, though, that the scenarios have a focus on what will be the situation in three to five years' time, depending on the chosen time horizon. Each scenario should be written describing the environment which has been achieved for that scenario at the end of the time period. It is as if the reality of that future is being described in words enticing the community to engage in the outcomes of that scenario. The tenses of the language need to be written in the sense that 'we are now in this future which we had planned'. Take the reader of the scenario forward in time and create that sense of being there in that future.

This future orientation of the writing can be helped with phrases such as: 'The Library in 2011 continues to be ...'. Other approaches might be to describe the environment which has been achieved in that future frame: 'The University community has engaged rapidly and completely with the possibilities of digital communication, access and work. The students actually prefer to work completely from their laptops ...'. Other issues which the scenarios envisaged might be described as: 'The organisation's innovative focus has also led to its recent strategic alliance with an innovative ... multi-media web company. Partnerships and commercially strategic alliances represent major opportunities, and a major direction, for this organisation and its customers.' So different phrases and the use of positive achievement-orientated language can sell the particular scenario as an environment which has been achieved, albeit in the imagination of the workshop participants. The scenarios can be written more simply in terms of the relevance of the library to their own community: 'Community and academic coffers have been depleted by crisis responses to a general economic decline along with decreased tax revenue. Funding for libraries is less available.' This is a very valid descriptive approach setting a scene. In this case the words were created before the economic crisis which began in late 2008.

This highlights the relevance of this imaginative approach. Another line: 'The library offers learning programmes that are in high demand by the local community and faculty alike.' The style of the writing and the actual approach can be designed for the community and purpose of the scenario planning process. Reading the scenario should evoke the feeling that the reader is in the described environment.

It is ideal to share the resulting scenarios back to the participants to gain feedback and to achieve a validation that the written scenarios are what were intended. Any feedback is useful and helpful and can be included in one way or another.

A decision has to be made at this point as to how to move from three scenarios to achieving the 'Preferred Scenario'. This will be handled differently by each organisation conducting this process. The choice will be affected by the political situation, the sense of urgency in the organisation for a new future and/or the size of the community and the difficulty in communicating with that wider community. One library may use the three scenarios and establish a poster campaign to gain further feedback from the community of users as to what they see as being important in each scenario and to what scenario they are attracted. Another library may take the three scenarios to discussions with senior academic and student groups across the campus to gain feedback. This is an excellent opportunity to have the library issues and futures widely discussed on campus, while portraying a vibrant and active library leadership. A consortium organisation may establish a 'roadshow', taking the futures to the 'owners' of the organisation and seeking their reactions in their own home environments. There are, of course, many other processes which could be designed to meet particular circumstances. It may be that the organisation decides to merge the three scenarios internally without further external debate. From any of these processes the feedback can assist a small group into the final phase: to construct the Preferred Scenario.

7. Create the Preferred Scenario

In writing this final Preferred Scenario it is good to remember that this document will stand as a benchmark against which the future performance of the library organisation will be measured. It must be written to set the reader in the target year by which the Scenario is to be achieved. This is not what the organisation is going to achieve but what it *has* achieved. This orientation is critical. The next chapter will discuss where to go and what to plan once the Preferred Scenario has been agreed to. However, once the final feedback has been achieved, the Preferred Scenario will not just be one of the futures but will, to some extent, include aspects of a number of them. It will predominantly be one of the scenarios but it will include features gained from the other two. So it is not a matter of just choosing one future but of stretching the organisation's capacity for risk and innovation in their future. The graph on page 122 highlights the need to place the Preferred Scenario as being strong on Future Focus and also Strategic Thinking. With this positioning, a challenging and exciting scenario can be created.

Notes

1. Toffler, A. (2010) Available at: *http://thinkexist.com/quotes/alvin_toffler* (accessed on 20 July 2010).
2. There are other examples now being used. A recent example is the 'Bookends Scenarios' developed for the Public Library section of the State Library of NSW. Available at: *http://www.sl.nsw.gov.au/services/public_libraries/publications/docs/bookendsscenarios.pdf* (accessed on 20 January 2010).
3. The titles of the stakeholders will vary in each library sector.

7

Scenarios and implementation

This chapter

The journey of creating a scenario or a new story about your organisation is almost complete and with that a new process is to begin. This chapter will deal with the successful implementation and the sustenance of that achievement. There will be a discussion of the major issues to be mindful of and the more 'left-field' disruptive issues which may impact on the organisation.

Preferred Library Scenario

The preceding chapters have enabled us to arrive at a word description of the future we want for our organisation in say three to five years' time. Key elements of the Preferred Scenario have also been identified. A good example of these elements is included in the Preferred Scenario for the Hong Kong Polytechnic University. These Key Elements will assist both in the marketing and in the strategic planning. It has had a great deal of input from various people, users, stakeholders and staff. The Preferred Library Scenario is a document to be proud of as it articulates a shared community view of the future the organisation is now being directed toward. A great investment has been made in this document and therefore there needs to be a strong return on that investment.

There are any number of ways in which the Preferred Library Scenario can be used. It is essentially a tool for marketing, a strategic planning filter, and a broad roadmap.

Marketing

An integral part of the Preferred Library Scenario should be the title of the Scenario. The title should be imaginative and marketable. The examples in the case studies in Chapter 9 bear witness to this: The Learning Village; Moving to the Front of House; The Learning Hub. The title should describe in a few words what the essence of the scenario is. This title will become synonymous with the work which will proceed to achieve the Preferred Scenario.

The most essential marketing step is to have the Preferred Scenario validated by the most senior person in the organisation to which the library belongs. This will give the authority of the organisation to the Preferred Scenario, as being the accepted future for the library. This is a vital initial part of the marketing effort. Beyond this a marketing plan should be drafted so that the scenario and the library's future intentions can be made plain to everyone. Remember in this process that the best groups who will support your plans are the members of the focus groups and scenario construction groups who have helped to contribute to and to construct the scenario. They are in a sense your 'Scenario Alumni'. They are a powerful group to re-enlist over the next few years and to further sell the scenario across your organisation.

The initial marketing can be very simple. It can be as simple as having a 'roadshow' visiting every faculty or group in your community. In the case of a consortium, it may be taking the scenario to groups of member libraries across the geographic boundaries of the consortium for wide ranging input and discussion. Roadshows are very effective devices, marketing what has been done and then gaining support for the strategic resourcing of action plans emanating from the scenario. Both outcomes are important in the short and medium terms. The Roadshow can be formal, whereby visits are organised to stakeholder groups in the institution or community. They can be informal as well, with displays in the library or around the community spaces.

Strategic planning

The Preferred Scenario needs to be put into action and this is where the strategic planning tool comes into play. If scenario planning has identified the future, then strategic planning will help to allocate the resources and establish the plans by which that future can be met.

The translation of the Preferred Scenario into a Strategic Plan needs identification of the key elements in the scenario. This can be done by analysing what forces came out of the scenario processes and were finally articulated in the Preferred Scenario. Typically there will be eight to ten major forces. These areas of focus will sharpen the Strategic Plan. These will effectively be the main strategic areas for the near future. Some of these Elements may be within a grouping such as Learning or Building. But the elements will emerge as strategic action areas in a plan and will need to attract funding for their successful implementation. It is not the intention of this book to describe the Strategic Plan processes except to say that the plans will emerge from the scenarios as necessary actions in order to meet the scenario. Looking at the various scenarios in the case studies in Chapter 9, it is instructive to look at the emerging elements.

Using the Hong Kong Polytechnic Scenario it became clear that there were nine key elements. They were: Outreach, Print Value, Research Involvement, Integral Contribution to the Institution's programmes, Sustainability, Everywhere, Digital Lives, Avatar Librarians, and Social Spaces. These headings broadly described what the Scenario was describing. It was especially the case that the strategic was driven by the need for the library to be everywhere; to be as digital as it could, even using avatar librarians; to outreach to its clients; and to create social spaces in which print would integrate with the digital in a sustainable environment.

These key elements were eventually grouped into six strategic areas which were: Collection Development; Learning and Teaching Engagement; Research Enhancement; Communication and Promotion; Partnership Development; and The Skilling of our People. While the strategic areas have been very effective they would never have driven the scenario. The imagination in the scenario drove the vision and the future. The Strategic Plan is translating that imagination into reality.

Roadmap

As a roadmap, the Preferred Scenario should be used in all the planning documents for budget, quality, staffing or capital. It is also important to find expression in the requests for the funds needed for operations, of the quality ambitions, of the skills and staff needed to achieve the Preferred Library Scenario (PLS) and of the capital needed for equipment and physical buildings. As that roadmap, it should be referred to often, so that all are aware of the document and what it foresees. It should also be used for review purposes in each year beyond the articulation of the Scenario. It should be a constant testing board. It is good to remind everyone of what is being achieved over time that was articulated in the Scenario. 'Why did the library create a softer and warmer collaborative learning environment?'; 'Why did the library create a coffee shop?'; 'Why are we structuring the library staffing in this way?'; 'Why are we removing books from the library and storing them collaboratively with books from other libraries?' The answer is simple: it is because the Community articulated them in the Preferred Library Scenario. That the Community was behind the Preferred Scenario and its many elements is a very strong indicator of support. It would be clear to anyone observing the process that the 'community' perhaps did not want *all* the elements in the scenario, but various forces wanted one aspect or another. The scenario is clever in that it can coalesce these various forces into one vision. It is apparent that it is impossible to direct cats in one direction but it is possible to herd cats into a general direction. The scenario process can balance and harmonise apparently contradictory forces into the one direction. It is also an excellent vehicle for change, allowing users and staff to move gently yet firmly from one position into the future.

Keeping the scenario alive

The Preferred Scenario will not 'live' for ever. After eighteen months to two years the Preferred Scenario should be reviewed, not to revitalise the Scenario itself but to review what has been achieved in a strategic sense; what has not happened and what needs to happen. In such a strategic review, it will be instructive how much has been achieved and in what ways. It will also be noticed how much change has happened that was anticipated and how much that was not anticipated. Remember from Chapter 1 that the future is not linear but that decision points along the way drive us in one direction or another. Within the preparation time of this book, the global financial crisis settled on all our plans like an enveloping glue, slowing everything down and making previously possible plans near impossible or at least severely postponed. Chapter 8 of this book will talk about the roadblocks along the path to the final implementation of the Preferred Scenario. It will discuss the issues of chance and worst case scenarios affecting the final shape of the organisation, its services and staff.

Mid-term review

The mid-term review will hearten staff who have put so much energy into making it all happen. They will be heartened by looking backwards and realising what has been achieved. Sometimes the achievement will not be what was intended, and it may be at a tangent to what was conceived. An example of this might be where a complete revitalisation of a building might have been intended whereas only a partial project could be achieved. This is not a problem of the desired scenario but rather a reality of the organisation's financial or implementation capability. Another example might be where the scenario called for the construction of a coffee shop. During the implementation it may become clear that this will not be possible to achieve in the short term for a variety of reasons. An alternative might, however, be possible. A coffee cart parked outside the library may be readily achievable as a first step toward the ultimate achievement. The scenario may have called for the organisation to grow in certain directions. The growth may not have been what had been envisaged but has resulted in amalgamations with other similar organisations to create a different but nonetheless powerful organisation.

The point is that, in the phase of implementation, the reality will, more than likely, be different, but in the same or a similar vein to what had been foreseen. So a formal mid-term review is very desirable to ensure that the organisation is on track or that it needs adjustment or that particular areas need more emphasis or resources. It is mostly the case that resources are not overly abundant in any organisation but it is the management of the resources which is critical. It will require considerable focus on the part of the organisation's management team to keep a sharp eye on what was intended to be achieved. Despite the vagaries of day-to-day operational concerns and issues, it is crucial to stay focused.

The convening of the 'Scenario Alumni' could be a useful occasion to deliver a Report Card on the perceived and actual performance. The report card could be structured in any of a number of ways and delivered in a variety of ways in a workshop or cocktail occasion. This would be a different exercise to a Business Plan or Strategic Plan report. It is a re-assembling of those who had the initial imagination; who saw all the pieces of the different scenarios merge into a Preferred Scenario. They will deliver a warm critical view of what has been achieved. They will also reinvigorate the Strategic Plan to achieve the Preferred Scenario but, just as importantly, they will re-ignite the enthusiasm in the Community for what it was envisaged would be achieved.

The staff in the implementation of the Preferred Scenario

In any review such as is described above there is inevitably a re-positioning of the staff resources within the organisation. The staff are an organisation's primary and most important resource. It is the only way in which objectives can be achieved. We have talked in earlier chapters about the effect of change on staff and users alike. In some ways change has a different dimension for each group. The user community may be characterised as wanting change more strongly at the service end while the staff may be characterised as wanting change in a more carefully measured manner. So the gap between the two groups on a continuum of change could be great and growing. Change in the structure and role of a library staff is important if the organisation is to meet the scenario articulated by the user community in the Preferred Scenario. This change will not take place overnight but over a period of years as the organisation is adjusting to a new purpose. The Strategic Plans set in place after the construction of the Preferred Scenario would have created new actions for the organisation and with these actions would have come the need for new skills and staff, and actions which did not occupy them previously.

This mid-term review will provide an opportunity to understand both how the staff still feel about the Preferred Scenario and how they are going about changing their roles, their work and their view of the library in their community. Peter Sidorko, in the final chapter of this book, talks about change and its impact on an organisation from a practical and theoretical perspective. As Sidorko says: 'The process of getting people involved in developing the preferred scenario that actually does result in a satisfactory outcome and a sense of ownership by participants is not the end of the journey.'[1]

The Preferred Scenario will be a unifying force among the library staff. It will enable those who want the library to move to a new model to see that vision articulated in the Preferred Scenario. It will also assist those who were reluctant to see change to move gradually toward this new future. This document will draw people together through the business of actually constructing the future.

Note

1. Sidorko, P. (2010). *See* Chapter 10 of this volume, p. 189.

8

Choice, chance and (less than) certainty

This chapter

Before we look at some case studies and consider the impact of change on an organisation, this chapter will conclude the process of establishing the Preferred Scenario, but start the process by which the skills we have learnt are translated into our own future behaviours. In this, these final words set out to create a mindset for how we view our future after we have completed the Preferred Scenario. There will be a discussion about what to look for in our environment and we will conclude with a review of the major issues which seem to be looming on the horizon. Through all of our days ahead we will be dealing with the three Cs. We will have less than Certainty, we will experience Chance and random events which will affect us greatly, but through it all we will have Choice.

Chance and randomness

A wonderfully entertaining and thoughtful book by Leonard Mlodinow entitled *The Drunkard's Walk: How randomness rules our lives* should be one of our personal guides to the future. 'The greatest challenge in understanding the role of randomness in life is that although the basic principles of randomness arise from everyday logic, many of the consequences that follow from those principles prove counterintuitive.'[1] Mlodinow offers a number of examples to illustrate the power of random events. One concerns the baseball careers of Babe Ruth and Roger Maris. One could equally translate this example into the sports of cricket, ice hockey or whatever. Babe Ruth in his career had established a season high number of home runs at 60 in a season. Nobody had broken that record. Then in a remarkable season Roger Maris and Mickey Mantle slugged it out to beat the Babe Ruth record. Maris succeeded in hitting 61 home runs in a season. Maris's career both before and afterwards never came close to the magical figure of 60 home runs. He had never hit more than 39 home runs in a season. He was clearly a good player but his performance excelled in that one season which he was never able to replicate. It all came together for him. Mlodinow demonstrates through the use of statistics that his extraordinary performance can be explained as much by chance as by other orderly explanations about talent and training.[2] As Mlodinow says, 'When we look at extraordinary accomplishments in sports – or elsewhere – we should keep in mind that extraordinary events can happen without extraordinary causes. Random events often look like nonrandom events, and in interpreting human affairs we must take care not to confuse the two. Though it has taken centuries, scientists have learned to look beyond apparent order and recognize the hidden randomness in both nature and everyday life.'[3]

Arguments have ensued for years about why Maris was able to succeed in one season but never again. These explanations include fear of failure, injury and also being unable to cope with success. The record performance, however, can as readily be explained by random events. So this evidences how our view of the past and of the future can be shaped by false understandings rather than by a simpler explanation as a random event. 'If the details we are given fit our mental picture of something, then the more details in a scenario, the more real it seems and hence the more probable we consider it to be – even though any act of adding less-than-certain details to a conjecture makes the conjecture less probable.'[4] There is a clear inconsistency between probability theory and our own interpretation of our futures – an area of uncertainty. This does not mean that we cannot work at predicting the future but it does add notes of caution as we move on from our Preferred Scenario.

Mlodinow explains that 'The probability that two events will both occur can never be greater than the probability that each will occur individually.'[5] He provides various examples drawn from the literature of psychology and statistics to illustrate this. They are worth reading if you are interested in these laws of probability. From our perspective, it is the case that we try to interpret the future by what we consider to be the more likely and yet the cues which we take from our world are often skewed by our experiences and interpretation of what is probable. The necessary skill to develop is to recognise that we do skew our predictions and to understand the effect which this will have on what we decide. It is also important not to close one's mind to what could be possible.

Mlodinow relates the famous case of the columnist Marilyn vos Savant, renowned for being the person with the highest recorded IQ of 228.[6] She was commenting on the issue of probability in the television game *Let's Make a Deal*. The contestant winning the show was asked to choose their prize by selecting the prize behind one of three doors. This is also called *The Monty Hall Problem*. Behind two of the doors was nothing, while the real prize was behind the third door.

If the contestant chose one door and then the host of the programme opened one of the remaining doors to reveal that it contained no prize, should the contestant change the choice which was already made? Marilyn vos Savant said that the contestant should change the choice to the other remaining choice. Mathematicians across the country all came out to say that she had got her advice wrong. Nobody stood by Marilyn. In fact, she was correct and yet it took a long time for this to be accepted publicly.[7] The seemingly obvious solution that there was now a 50/50 chance of success, having had one of the choices negated, was wrong. Yet all the experts howled and berated this columnist. The point of this story here is not in the solution but that so many people fell into line with each other to deride vos Savant: a group-thinking position.

The most obvious answer is not necessarily the correct one. So it is important not to be blinded by the tyranny of the expert or, more especially, the tyranny of many voices. The issue of what is most probable or least probable can be seen as a statistical exercise but also should be recognised as a problem when predicting the future. The Monty Hall Problem illustrates the careful application of logic in the world of probability. To choose correctly in this game is to win on average 66 per cent more often than those who saw the probability as being 50 per cent. To increase one's chances of success in any enterprise is always highly desirable. To recognise the application of probability and the role of chance will be crucial in maintaining the future tracking of the Library or Information Service.

The game of chess is an excellent training ground for predicting the future or at least working toward it. The mental training of working to plan a move and to understand the range of options open to your opponent is very worthwhile. The mental exercise to then try and predict the range of your future moves with the corresponding range of options open to your opponent becomes more and more complex. It is less easy to see the future in this forward-looking exercise than it is to see the past reasons or mistakes in the game of chess. Nonetheless, the application and mental rigour of a chess game is an excellent discipline to good thinking, planning and application of probability.

Adoption of risk

To be successful we have to be open to failure. To be able to predict the future we have to have experienced failure. We have different tolerances for risk which can be individually based or even cultural. We all engage in risk every day in many more ways than we are conscious of. But it is the role of risk and the society's attitude toward risk which is of interest here. Sociologists would argue that risk is being treated differently now socially than, say, thirty years ago. Ulrich Beck indeed believes that our society had become a risk society and this view has influenced much of the thinking relating to risk and uncertainty.[8] Most often we identify risk in order to avoid it altogether but we can always choose a level of risk. The notion of risk is important in terms of our aspiration to control it and to therefore better predict the future.

> If you want to succeed, double your failure rate. (IBM Pioneer Thomas J. Watson[9])

If we had only certainty in our world there would be no risk, but we have uncertainty into the future and therefore there are various levels of risk. If we cannot eliminate risk we have to deal with it in our lives and organisations. Risk management is practised in order to reduce the probability of known risk and difficulties. But where events and technologies are changing so rapidly, it is difficult as we are dealing with higher levels of uncertainty. Jakob Arnoldi emphasises that 'risks are not *actual* but rather *potential* dangers'.[10] The risks we are dealing with are disruptive across a range of industries allied to libraries. Thinking about the issues in this chapter in these terms might link for us the concepts of risk and uncertainty. We can decide the levels of both that we can tolerate; and what is probable and that which is not.

This chapter thus far has looked at the role of probability and chance as we might experience it in the future. So it is useful in what remains of this section of the book to look at some of the issues which will most likely have some significant impact on our futures in our endeavours. There are a few issues which will need to be heeded in the near future.

Issue 1: abundance of data

The abundance of data is overwhelming the world. The amount of data being collected in the world is astronomical. 'Wal-Mart, a retail giant, handles more than 1 million customer transactions every hour, feeding databases estimated at more than 2.5 petabytes – the equivalent of 167 times the books in America's Library of Congress. ... The world contains an unimaginably vast amount of digital information which is getting vaster ever more rapidly.'[11] The volume of data is causing huge environmental difficulties with the amount of water being consumed just to keep the computer centres able to keep their vast banks of servers in air-conditioned comfort. The amount of heat being generated by computers is rising beyond all expectation, especially in a world suffering increasing scarcity of water.

The data, at the same time, offers confusion with how to comprehend what it means and also significant opportunities to understand what users are doing with the data. The data is creating new business models for those who can use the data to comprehend what it is reflecting. Google is one obvious example, where they have been able to harness the data using their PageRank algorithm counting the number of links from other website pages coming to this particular website. This was a significant departure from the previous counts of words on individual web pages to ascertain the 'relevance' of particular searches. Google keep much of what they learn from our searches across their search engine secret, in that it has real economic value to the advertisers who contribute much of their tens of billions of income annually. Over 99 per cent of their income is derived from advertising, although Google handles only half of the world's Internet searches. Clearly, company logistical operations have benefited enormously from the powerful use of computers to predict the location for and need of particular product lines from their customers. It is reported that for just one ingredient, vanilla, Nestlé was able to reduce the number of specifications and use fewer suppliers, resulting in a saving of $30 million each year.[12] So it is the case with many logistics operations globally.

The business of using words as data is very small indeed. Researchers at the University of California (San Diego) examined the flow of data to American households. They found that in 2008 such households were bombarded with 3.6 zetabytes[13] of information (or 34 gigabytes per person per day). An alarming example is the calculation of 'A Day in the Life of an E-mail'. What starts out as a 1.1 MB message sent to four people will convert to 51.5 MB at the end of the day as it is stored, transmitted and backed up. The more

| **Figure 8.1** | How 3.6 zettabytes of data get consumed |

Evolution of reading

Fraction-of words NIFO_w form different sources

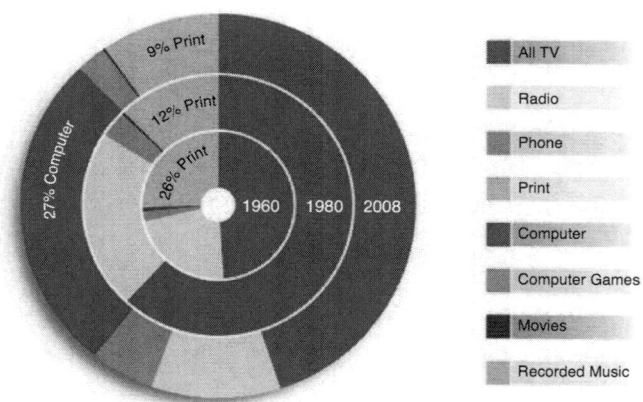

Source: http://gizmodo.com/5423599/how-36-zettabytes-of-data-get-consumed (accessed 6 April 2010)

responses to the message and the longer the conversation trails the worse the situation becomes.[14]

The biggest data hogs were video games and television. In terms of bytes, written words are insignificant, amounting to less than 0.1 per cent of the total.[15] However, the amount of reading people do, previously in decline because of television, has almost tripled since 1980, thanks to all that text on the Internet.[16] This is a limited study, not taking into account the business use of words as data. So data is important but words are not in the total context.

But even while the amount of word bytes is relatively small, we know so little about our user behaviours and interests. Among librarians there has been an emphasis on the use of the Integrated Library Systems (ILS) with very little understanding of what is happening and virtually no understanding of what is happening with e-serials and now e-books. This is despite the fact that many libraries are now committing around 75 per cent of their acquisitions budgets to digital resources. Libraries need to investigate and understand what information behaviours are being exhibited. They need the equivalent of the Google business model invention of moving from word counts per page to counts of inbound websites. They need to move away from the very limited MARC descriptors of books to the types of searches which the users are using on the Internet. They need to partner with publishers in understanding the metrics of library content usage.

Issue 2: search engine capability

The immaturity of library search engines and the data structures which they search is of immense concern to all librarians. Research has clearly indicated that the first place for users to search is not the library's OPAC, or computer catalogue. The library as a place of first resort is slipping.

This is partly due to the phenomenon of Google/Yahoo and their powerful search algorithms; sophisticated search engines giving the user 'what they want' or at least 'what they accept'. They do this even by recording mistakes and giving access to the correct term or spelling but also by anticipating need. This 'push' capability is evident in systems such as Amazon, which provides related materials to the search while building histories of interested searches and possible materials of interest. These search systems obviously have huge computing capacity behind them but they have a fundamentally different approach or philosophy toward searching. In a time when all materials were in print, the catalogue served the purpose of allowing users to both search for groups of materials under subject headings but also pointing the user to a class or location number where further searching could occur on the shelves where books of a similar nature were clustered. Libraries have not fundamentally changed this search model but rather have incrementally built on this model. It is becoming increasingly unwieldy and creaking under the pressures of a digital environment.

The ILS (Integrated Library System) search engine is limited to searching the library's collections of books while the metadata is limited to the MARC record search fields and a structured vocabulary. The terms which many of our users use are much more free-ranging and not limited to a structured language of subject headings. The newer search tools allow for user tagging, where additional search terms can be added to the item record. This is obviously good but it is an 'after-the-event' effort. The native searching of a wider set of terms is important to achieve the benefits of a structured language approach to the description of print and digital objects but also the natural searching behaviours of our library users.

Federated searching across different platforms or silos of information is a certain improvement but is still very clunky as this mode of searching struggles to deal with different proprietary systems. Federated searching and the use of standards such as Z39.50 have improved the integration of print and subscribed or owned digital resources significantly but much remains to be done to create seamless searching. It is ironic that a search tool such as Google Scholar yields good results for the user in a particular institution but, mostly, the end user scarcely realises how they have come to gain access to these resources. The situation feels to me as if our search systems are in transition to better ways which will yield easier and fuller access for our users.

Issue 3: avoid group thinking

It is always very difficult to be the lone voice in a crowded room. It takes a clear head with a strong background of thinking and research to have a view which is worth defending, especially when it is different to the prevailing view. It takes courage and commitment. Most often it does not come to this. Most often it is the case that there may be two views, with most people accepting the prevailing view and not working hard enough to question the existing view or to understand the newer or different view. It is often easier just to accept the 'status quo'. Perhaps this is not directly 'group thinking' but it is dangerous. At another level it is stagnating thinking.

The danger of group thinking is that conversations between colleagues are too much in synch with each other. No external ideas or challenges are allowed into this mode of thinking. Various examples of where this has become dangerous have been related earlier in this book. No other explanation for a phenomenon can be entertained. In this circumstance different ideas are not even accepted or tested for relevance. There are a number of ways by which this problem can be managed and avoided.

It is important to read outside one's own literature for social and technological developments, ideas, approaches to problems, solutions and challenges. An interesting aspect of our library operations is now the employment of people from different discipline backgrounds to help the organisation grow. A community of professionals! But in employing programmers, database managers, marketers, trainers, learning consultants, graphic artists and so on, do we allow these people to be part of the professional library planning and operational cultures? Do we allow them to question and to provoke different thinking? Why does the library do something? Why does it approach an issue in a particular manner? Does the library understand that users or groups of users think differently to the prevailing understanding which the library culture sees is the case? Why not try a different software? Why not push information to particular client groups?

If group thinking is stagnating in cerebral terms, the employment of different professional groupings is 'eye-opening', if we allow it to be. Admit the ideas and perceptions which these different professional groupings offer. Openly accept and discuss their ideas and observations. Their incorporation into the library culture or view of the world will open new insights but will also include and commit them to the library and its Preferred Scenario.

One final aspect of group thinking is to challenge our professional staff as they grow longer into their careers, when they may not be thinking as freshly as they once did. The emerging generational change can be a source of frustration for both the older and younger generations but it can also be a way of creating a stimulating and exciting culture of ideas and ambitions for the Preferred Scenario. Tensions are wonderful if managed correctly. Tensions can be between different generations or between different discipline groups in the employ of the library. As said earlier in this book, the library we are managing and designing is for future generations. It is a matter of blending new ideas and approaches with the intuition and experience of the management.

Issue 4: learn to take risks

Is risk a bad thing? What is risk? Can we achieve much with risk or without risk?

Risk is a peculiar thing. We do not live without risk at some level. We live because we risk. We risk to live! Much of what is being said about risk is perhaps not acknowledged as risk. Risk is not concerned with the past. Risk is future-focused. The achievement of any future is concerned with the management of risk. If a reference were drawn to the title of the book discussed earlier, *The Drunkard's Walk*, someone under the influence of alcohol is scarcely concerned with risk. Alcohol reduces awareness of risk, or any of its threats or benefits. Intoxicated people are the most risk-tolerant of all. As library managers we will individually relate to risk to varying degrees, as much measured by our individual personalities and attributes. But risk will present itself to us and our response to it will determine outcomes.

Risk is, for the most part, associated with disaster or catastrophe. It is also seen to reflect the worst-case scenario; the scenario which none of us wishes to see realised. When dealing with uncertainty, as described earlier in this chapter, the choice of different levels and shades of risk will surely try us. Yet whenever money is given and invested, whether in a 'bottom-line' company or a not-for-profit service, all the elements of business activity are involved.[17] There are many consortia in existence across the globe now. One of the best experiences any budding manager can have is to move from an expenditure-based organisation such as a library to an income-based organisation such as a not-for-profit organisation. The experience really does instil a real sense of what risk is, especially in uncertain times. The birth and growth of Lyrasis[18] is a very good example of using scenario planning and the management of uncertainty.

Issue 5: continue to build a trust metric for the library

Trust is a vital aspect of all communication. If the source of the information being communicated is not trusted, neither will the information be. Trust is vital for publishers and for libraries. Publishers establish trust in their brand name as being respectable and authoritative. What follows is that books which they publish bear that authority. If a publisher has to withdraw a title because of plagiarism or other falsehoods, then there is a severe loss of reputation and trust.

The advent of the Internet has made huge amounts of information available, but very little of it is authoritative. So is material found on the Internet trustworthy? Well, much of it is clearly relayed without a known process by which the material gains authority. If there is no peer review process or respected publisher with their editorial processes then it is dangerous to assume that the material can be trusted.

Libraries have always been trusted organisations. They have been branded trustworthy in their own right as well as for the materials which they have made available. By extension, librarians are a trusted profession. But the Internet is creating unease in the community with these relationships. The Internet content is being accepted by many as valid even when it is plainly not. Libraries need to understand what business they are in. Newspapers thought that they were in the business of allowing people to advertise rather than helping people to sell things. This is a paradox.

There are two responses to this issue. Firstly, there is an educative aspect – a clear role for the librarian is to instruct in the ways by which content can be evaluated for authenticity. Secondly, there is a new role emerging by which web content could be stamped with a Kitemark.[19] Trust is, as Kieron O'Hara has pointed out, 'a wider attitude toward people and institutions that can as suddenly appear as disappear'.[20]

The issue of trust is a risk factor in the future of a library. It can be lost or could be extended into new realms. As indicated above, the risk of doing nothing is more dangerous than that of adopting new approaches. The reputation of trust in the library organisation and profession is at risk if one does nothing.

Issue 6: so what is *your* future?

In the final analysis, choice is with us through all the analysis and the articulation of futures in a Preferred Scenario. That future will not remain constant but will change and mutate. This final issue is effectively about making choices after the Preferred Scenario has been proclaimed and is in the process of being implemented.

A recent report on the challenges for academic libraries in difficult economic times reports that:

> After a decade of growth in budgets and services, librarians now expect a sustained period of cuts. Library budgets have risen over the past ten years – although not as much as overall university income and expenditure – as both the volume and range of library services have expanded. Librarians from across the higher education (HE) sector now expect budget cuts over the next three years.
>
> The scale of the cuts means that libraries must rethink the kinds and levels of service they provide in support of their universities' missions. The scope for further simple efficiency savings is small, and so librarians are having to think more strategically about:
>
> ■ *the balance of expenditure on information resources on the one hand, and staffing on the other.* The balance varies significantly across the sector, and there is a close relationship between staffing and service levels;

- *whether and if so how to sustain existing kinds and levels of services while at the same time developing new services to meet new needs.* Many libraries across the sector are considering cuts in services; but they need to ensure that staff focus more on user-facing functions, and to develop a more detailed understanding of the costs of their activities;

- *the squeeze on book budgets, and how to meet the student demand for core texts.* E-books could help ease this problem, but publishers' policies on pricing and accessibility are inhibiting take-up; and

- *the costs and sustainability of current levels of journal provision.* Cancelling large numbers of titles or a whole big deal will give rise to considerable opposition. But librarians are looking at various options to reduce the costs of their current portfolios.[21]

What has been learnt through this whole process is the need to research, to maintain a weather eye within the field of our own profession but also elsewhere. Most importantly we have learnt to collaborate and to be empowered by being open and sharing data and future positions. Tapscott and Williams, in their book *Wikinomics*, called it 'collaborative minds: the power to think differently'.[22] Among their arguments is that we are seeing the end of intellectual property as ideas and data are shared for greater effect and outcome. Certainly libraries need open-source solutions to be able to share the digital information they subscribe to and create. The traditional partnerships of the past still infiltrate our thinking about library and vendor: the vendor will do and libraries will service. Ken Haycock also highlights that the 'public good' is being replaced by *public value*.[23] So return on investment (ROI) arguments are very important but extremely difficult in library environments to successfully operate. Collaborative librarianship is what I might describe not as doing it ourselves but having a genuine partnership of addressing disruption and creating new arrangements. This is a leadership where libraries shape what is to be delivered and how it is delivered in new partnership arrangements. It is proactive redefining of collection development which is the most pressing issue of the early years of the twenty-first century.

Decisions will be improved through being open and collaborative, with new skills being required to achieve the best futures out of this mode of thinking. Much research is happening into the processes of decision-making. Much as this book has advocated leaving decisions until the end in the process of creating scenarios, so too Thaler and Sunstein say that 'by insisting that choices remain unrestricted, we think that the risks of inept or even corrupt designs are reduced'.[24] Do not rush to locked-in leadership positions; leadership is more about creating the opportunities and the belief that the future is strong even if a little unclear.

Improving decision-making strategies in our libraries is a good way to bring the earlier issues into a framework which Thaler and Sunstein call their *choice architecture*. This is but one tool available through the literature. Their argument that people make the best decisions by leaving the strategic open as long as feasible is good, allowing for what they call 'nudges' rather than hard commitments one way or another. Nudging has a certain leadership flair to it as people can be nudged from one position to another while allowing an understanding of what is happening in their environment.

Conclusion

It is not intended to be prescriptive in bringing this part of the book to a close. The lessons of this work lie in the power of our imagination, our awareness of the impact of disruptive influences on our business models and what we might do to prepare for new futures. That is the simple message.

Clinging to 'the way we did it' is an almost instant recipe for disaster. The best solution for your organisation is not mine to determine, although this book might help you in your deliberations. The future is a wonderful and seductive mix of enticement and threat; it is alluring and it is frightening; in the end, we should all embrace it, for if you do not it will most certainly pass you by. Come on the journey. It will be exhilarating!

Notes

1. Mlodinow, L. (2008). *The Drunkard's Walk: How randomness rules our lives.* London: Penguin Books, p. 7.
2. The performances covered in this baseball example are difficult to replicate in more recent baseball seasons that are contaminated by steroid abuse affecting performance.
3. Mlodinow, op. cit., p. 20.
4. Ibid., p. 24.
5. Ibid., p. 23.
6. A more complete explanation of this example is available at *http://en.wikipedia.org/wiki/Marilyn_vos_Savant* (accessed on 20 July 2010).
7. Available at: *http://en.wikipedia.org/wiki/Monty_Hall_problem* (accessed on 20 July 2010).
8. Beck, U. (1986/1992). *Risk Society: Towards a new modernity.* New Delhi: Sage. (Translated from the German Risikogesellschaft, published in 1986.)
9. Available at: *http://www.famousquotes.com/show/1049131* (accessed on 20 July 2010).
10. Arnoldi, J. (2009). *Risk: An Introduction.* Cambridge: Polity Press, p. 8.
11. 'Data, data everywhere' *The Economist* 394(8671) 27 February 2010, p. 3.

12. 'Special report on managing information', *The Economist* 394(8671) 27 February 2010, p. 6.

13. A zettabyte is equal to 1 billion terabytes. According to IDC, as of 2006 the total amount of digital data in existence was 0.161 zettabytes; the same paper estimates that by 2010, the rate of digital data generated worldwide will be 0.988 zettabytes per year. Mark Liberman calculated the storage requirements for all human speech ever spoken at 42 zettabytes, if digitised as 16 kHz 16-bit audio. This was done in response to a popular expression that states 'all words ever spoken by human beings' could be stored in approximately 5 exabytes of data (see exabyte for details). Liberman did 'freely confess that maybe the authors [of the exabyte estimate] were thinking about text.' Available at: *http://en.wikipedia.org/wiki/Zettabyte* (accessed on 20 July 2010).

14. Gantz, J. F. (2008). 'The diverse and exploding digital universe: An update forecast of worldwide information growth through 2011.' An IDC White Paper. March 2008.

15. Available at: *http://gizmodo.com/5423599/how-36-zettabytes-of-data-get-consumed* (accessed on 20 July 2010).

16. *The Economist*, op. cit., p. 5.

17. Haycock, K. (2008). 'Issues and trends' in Ken Haycock and Brooke E. Sheldon (eds), *The Portable MLIS: Insights from the experts*. Westport, CT: Libraries Unlimited, p. 204

18. Available at: *www.lyrasis.org* (accessed on 20 July 2010).

19. A *Kitemark* is a quality measure designed to assure consumers of safety and value. There are a number of systems already in existence mainly in manufacturing but imminent in education circles.

20. O'Hara, K. (2004). *Trust: From Socrates to spin*. Cambridge: Totem Books, pp. 282–3.

21. Challenges for academic libraries in difficult economic times: a guide for senior institutional managers and policy makers. Available at: *www.rin.ac.uk/system/files/attachments/Challenges-for-libraries-FINAL-March10.pdf*: 4.

22. Tapscott, D. and Williams, A. D. (2006). *Wikinomics: How mass collaboration changes everything*. London: Atlantic Books, p. 268.

23. Haycock, op. cit., p. 205.

24. Thaler, R. and Sunstein, C. (2009). *Nudge: Improving decisions about health, wealth and happiness*. London, Penguin, p. 12

9

Case studies

A number of case studies are replicated in this book. They are real examples of the power of scenarios. The scenarios presented in these case studies are options for different institutions, in different environments at different times.

Each case study is different. In a few instances, the background scenarios as well as the Preferred Library Scenario are presented. In other case studies, only the Preferred Library Scenario is presented.

Case study 1: A major Hong Kong university library

(As written by Steve O'Connor for the Hong Kong Polytechnic University Press)

Background

The Hong Kong Polytechnic University is the largest publicly-funded tertiary institution in Hong Kong in terms of number of students, with 26,000 full-time and part-time students (or 15,116 FTE) and an academic staff population of 1,128 FTE. It is an institution which is quickly evolving from one with a strong focus on excellence in teaching to that with a dual purpose of teaching and research. As such it is an institution in transition. This transition is in a higher education environment which is competitive within Hong Kong but increasingly within the wider context of the fast-developing mainland Chinese institutions. Further institutional pressures are to improve its position in the global rankings of institutions. These pressures create a variety of opportunities and difficulties for any library ordinarily but more so when considering the changes which all libraries are going through in the new digital environment. The PolyU Library was dealing with this situation in three languages: English, Cantonese and Putonghua. The situation in which this well-managed, staffed and resourced library was operating was complex. It needed to set new directions; it needed to determine its future with clarity; it needed to do all of this while bringing its user communities and senior university academics along on the journey. The library staff would always be the key change agents.

The management of the library understood the challenges facing them and elected to engage in a scenario planning process for a number of reasons. Firstly, the library wanted to engage the university community in choosing the options and directions for the future. Many changes were confronting the university, so it was crucial that the university management understood the opportunities facing them with regard to the positioning of their library.

Secondly, the library had been well managed with a long-standing management team. Early in 2007, the previous librarian had retired after 34 successful years in the position. Many of the staff had been with him for much of this period. With a new librarian in place it was felt important at one level to validate where the library was strategically but also to test the community and the wider environment as to where the library could be.

Thirdly, the scenario planning process was an excellent

opportunity to meet with the library's community to present the issues which confronted the library and also to explore the pressures within the academic and student communities. It was hoped to gain a clearer understanding on both sides of what was desirable and what was achievable.

Fourthly, it was hoped that this process would involve all the library staff and create in this group of nearly 160 persons an understanding of the library's position and the need to explore change. It was hoped to enlist all these people as agents of change as the process progressed.[1]

Preferred Library Scenario

The 'Learning Hub'

The PolyU Library in 2011 continues to be located on a land-locked campus, in the middle of one of the most densely populated parts of the world, but is now *everywhere else* at the same time. Its strong reputation for being busy is still true but it has successfully fused the information and study worlds; fused the physical and digital into one; fused locally produced and commercially produced information for the benefit of the University research community. This is a seamless world of quality information from the web, large sets of digital books and journals as well as great collections of books. The information is now even more digital and wherever possible print materials are delivered digitally. This is what is now called the LEARNING HUB for the students and researchers. The Library has focused its services more on outreach than previously. In reaching out it is both visiting the University community wherever it is and also bringing more of that same community to the revitalised Pao Yue-kong Library building. In this future, the traditional functions of the Library have been re-defined and re-focused to facilitate the growth of knowledge, collaborative learning, reflective thinking and institutional visibility.

A more comfortable and dynamic learning environment has been created to achieve the best problem-based learning situation whereby students can relax in lounge-type chairs to learn in relative comfort. These new facilities also encourage discussions and interactions between students in the same and differing discipline groups. It is a meeting place of *people and minds* which now includes both a quality coffee shop and small bookstore. This has created a new sense of energy and excitement. Exhibitions, performances and events also make this area a cultural hub of the campus. The Library's merging of information and people has made the campus a more vibrant place.

The lighting in many study carrels has now been tailored for the individual, thus creating a personalised study environment. Previous complaints about noise have been addressed in 2011 with the creation of more targeted discussions and interactive spaces. The study patterns and habits of each discipline are encouraged and supported in a library environment which has been architect re-designed with as many of the study needs in mind as possible. In all of this the Library has sought to be carbon-neutral, reducing its use of energy in many ways including programmes to reduce the consumption of paper and genuinely staying electronic. The Library and its users are leaders in this movement and have adopted and embraced the motto: 'Reduce, Reuse, Recycle'.

Not content with only the physical meeting spaces the Library has created new Facebook-type social spaces on the net in which information is being communicated and exchanged. Like its commercial cousin, the *PolyU Library-book* digital site has proven to be enormously popular as a *space* in which to navigate through in search of information. It is very relevant and in tune with the emerging groups of students who think, study and communicate very differently to the previous cohorts of students. Through this new style of library the students are finding masses of information which are both exciting and assisting their studies. The Library serves as an information gateway to staff, students, alumni and the wider community. It is difficult not to recognise the extent of the Library presence across the University. Virtual Librarians or avatars *roam* the Library web presences providing instant assistance. These 'Avatar Librarians', fluent in Putonghua, English and Cantonese, are instantly available to users on computer screens both on campus and remotely in the digital virtual information world. They have taken up the important role as information mentors. Information Literacy programmes, delivered both in physical and virtual space, prepare students for research at the University level, and to become successful life-long learners.

The Library has succeeded in creating boutique web spaces for each Faculty which are friendly and responsive to discipline interests. This has been especially well received in the lead-up to the creation of the 3-3-4 program. The users from each discipline feel that they have *a space or a place* to go to where they will be directly understood as they can speak their discipline language. The physical spaces in the Library have been made more personal, more conducive to learning and less anonymous.

The Library is very cognisant of the new students and has adjusted its systems to meet these new fluencies. A reputation has been gained by the Library for its anticipatory use of future technology, communication systems and devices. The LEARNING HUB lends itself now to a more active role in assisting learning and in partnering with different learning agencies on campus such as the Educational Development Centre. Informal discussions and collaborative group work are also more effective for the different study zones which have been created within the physical fabric of the Library building with the enhancement of Level 7. Those with learning disabilities find even more support.

The information available through the Library continues to be in both print and digital forms although the digital resources have grown very sharply from 2007. Support of the University's research effort has been focused more in close consultation with Faculty and University policy-makers. As a knowledge hub, the Library also collects all the research output of the University's Faculties and, in turn, highlights this work digitally to the University and importantly the World. The scope and richness of the important but lower-use research materials have increased markedly with the development of JURA as a HUCOM jointly-owned research repository. PolyU Library has strongly contributed to this important research centre. Hong Kong has maintained its strategic position as the regional information lighthouse. No country in this part of the world is able to match the academic resources now so readily accessible to Hong Kong academics.

This LEARNING HUB Library in 2011 is very much the kind of Library which was needed and sought by the members of the University community. They are proud of this new style of Library and the leading example it provides in Hong Kong and internationally.

Case study 2: A major Australian university library

(Kindly agreed to by Andrew Wells)

Background

This organisation had been very innovative in years past but with a very long-serving and stable staff who were reluctant to consider, let alone embrace, changed circumstances. The average age of this 200-member-plus staff was more than 57 years. The budget of the library was not as strong as in previous years and was under prospective challenge. The library's organisational structure into subject libraries located within a single physical building had been very innovative in its time but now found itself in a very different Internet world and lacking focus on a single strategic direction. Politics between various sections of the library made it difficult to move the library's purposes beyond a common grasp of the glories of the past. The new library leadership sought to examine new horizons and directions but found only resistance. The scenario planning process created three things. Firstly, by embracing the university community in a very public dialogue, the library staff was drawn slightly out of defensive postures to recognise some need to change. It became clear that the university community saw the library very differently to that of its well-established staff and expressed these views strongly. Secondly, the scenario planning process developed publicly (again) three viable scenarios for the future of the library. These futures were described not as futures which might be achieved but as different futures which had been realised in three years beyond the present time. In this way these choices, to some extent, were stark choices which the university administration and its library could choose to follow. Finally, by making this process very future-orientated and very public the community was empowered in a way in which it had never been engaged previously. This empowerment spoke loudly of the kind of digital world in which the library now found itself. It is clear that the digital world enables the individual to change much in their environment. So the engagement of the community in making choices was, at once, risky in a political sense but powerful in that through the process, the community felt that it was able to influence the direction of its library.

This Library embraced, at the end of this process, a scenario which was titled 'The Learning Village'. This very public articulation of a direction had been agreed to by the community and the administration. Library working groups went about the tasks of defining what these changes would mean. They described the effect which these changes would have on the staff that would be required to implement this new vision. The process had achieved much but, as much as a shirt worn inside out gives the viewer a very different view of the wearer, so it was for the library staff that had their views of the library turned inside out.[2]

Scenario 1

Not the present, but ...

The University Library opted to continue the path of growth to ensure that the collections are the main focus of the library's efforts ... something of which the University could be justifiably proud. The University Library sought to allow for the very significant expansion of space needed to accommodate the sizeable collection of resources with a rapidly declining capacity to house library users. The sizeable numbers of books and serials purchased from university resources, as well as from extensive donations (much of which is yet to be catalogued) had grown at such a rate, even with diminished financial resources, that the existing building had the lowest ranking for seat availability amongst university libraries in NSW.

The Library building has become a huge repository of materials with the disciplines physically separated in respective special libraries. The complexity of locating information in the Library has not been reduced. Limited space has been made available for computer work-stations and group study areas. Still users are seen wandering the corridors of shelving in search of materials. The staff profile is changing to meet the need for the collect and despatch services.

Finding it more and more difficult to meet the in-house technology needs of the information users, the Library compromised the competing demands of collections, staff and students with a less in-person service mode of operation. The profile of the Library on campus became more diffuse while seeking to ensure that as much information was available as possible.

The digital services have not totally replaced the physical collections and the formats of some information are available in physical and digital form. It became necessary, for space reasons, to locate the professional staff into the Faculties away from the Library itself. These staff provide course support as well as information literacy programs from within the Faculty structure. Information literacy training is carried out in the facilities of the Faculties because the Library has not been able to develop these spaces within its space priorities. The Library is constantly juggling service need, staff capacity and information acquisition. Budget priorities are complex with a mostly distributed staffing but a heavy requirement to service the vast collections spread across many floors.

The University Library's long tradition of innovation and responsiveness to academic and library user need has developed to this service model as a response to present priorities and an uncertain future.

Scenario 2

The Unseen Library

The University community has engaged rapidly and completely with the possibilities of digital communication, access and work. The students actually prefer to work completely from their laptops to engage with their curricula and to complete their subject assignments. They naturally wish to receive their subject outlines and other materials digitally while submitting their assignments in the same way. Their essays pass through electronic plagiarism detection in the process of being assessed. This is a new value-added service from the digital expertise of the Library. Many students rarely come onto the campus. They do so more for social than academic reasons.

The academic staff are in a similar position, working from home or their studies reliant on the Internet for professional stimulation and the exchange of information. Often their lectures are not delivered in person. The University Library has adapted to this by pruning its collections significantly to focus on the most highly used materials and providing as much as is possible online. It has consigned ownership of much of its pruned low-use collections to collaborative storage facilities that guarantee digital return of requested materials directly to the requesting user. It has also put into place effective partnerships enabling the library user to have unmediated access to a wider range of materials delivered digitally from a much larger 'collection' than had been previously 'owned' by the University. The users are very pleased with the power they have to request virtually anything and to have it delivered promptly to their desktop. In the highly competitive world of scholarly monographs the Library has negotiated deals to ensure a far better access within 24 hours than had previously been the case. This was achieved through collaborative profiling of academic research areas.

The users take information literacy courses online and have learnt to critically analyse, filter and navigate through the masses of information with the online assistance of librarians who are contracted to work from home, an office or wherever to assist the academic staff and students achieve excellence through information. A number of these services are available for a fee as a value-added service for the time-pressed coursework student. The Library staff skill mix is significantly different as they work to ensure the best information portal development. The information accessed is a complex web of contractual arrangements negotiated by skilled information professionals.

The lower cost per information unit has enabled the Library to invest more in navigation technologies, partnerships and resources than previously. It is now a truly 24/7 operation working closely with Faculties. It is occupying considerably less physical space than in previous years but, in other senses, is more pervasive.

Scenario 3

The Learning Village

Marshall McLuhan's axiom of 'learning a living' has been a profound driver for the operation of the new University Library. It has harnessed the capability of highly academically oriented people with the stimulation and excitement of ideas. It has built a learning space for the academic community where the power of digital and analogue information has been channelled in an interactive environment. The Library has created the spaces where true collaborative learning work occurs infused with the accessible relevant information. The sources of information are as broad as the user wishes them to be. They are not confined to one discipline or another. Ideas from philosophy have been seen to stimulate solutions in biology, while business colleagues have gained generic models from engineering structures. It has attracted international attention as a supportive strategy.

The learning interactions have seen collaborations between disciplines, previously distant, creating new areas of international research and student learning. These spaces are flexible but are comfortable for users of all levels and attitudes to feel at home. The spaces are thoughtfully equipped with wireless and other emerging technologies. The emphasis is on different uses of space rather than on discipline. This fertility carries seamlessly across in the Internet environment but has characteristics which are unique to the UNSW Learning Village.

Recognising that information needs are constantly changing, the *Learning Village* has established a network of information suppliers from both the commercial and educational sectors. All services are recognised as belonging to, although not necessarily provided by UNSW. Researchers know from experience that they now have access to a much more dynamic information environment stimulating serendipitous yet systematic discovery. The Learning Village nonetheless contributes most strongly to the provision of, and even creation of, scholarly information in Australasia/Asia.

The area is staffed by Info-Learning specialists (ILSs). Like the Learning Village, these professionals have outgrown older boundaries to respond to the challenges of not just retrieving information but setting it in contexts for educational use. They select services and information to further the educational and research impact of UNSW in the region. The measures of success are not in the volumes or serial titles owned but in information provided and solutions to problems addressed in the learning context. The research community thrive in this environment, finding stimulation in the relationship between teaching and research, and in the excitement of new insights into complex research problems. The students and researchers of this great University realise that while their own futures are not tied to the present or the past, neither is their University Library, which is responding in thoughtful and energetic ways.

Table 9.1 Atttributes of scenario outcomes

Attributes	'Steady as she goes'	The Unseen Library	The Learning Village
Collections	Owned ... analogue and digital but campus-based	Mostly access ... remotely sourced and digitally based	Owned high-use and access-contracted
Collection emphases	Departmental/ Faculty determined	Emphasis on electronic and not-in-person; most major digital databases	Service. Information institution-based; wide research support
Services	On-site for collection access; faculty-based for information literacy and course support	Contracted for delivery and cost; digital delivery whenever possible	Linked with teaching/ learning programmes and research emphases
Service emphasis	Legacy collections	Digital focus	Learning resources
Physical building	Collection needs to expand; little space for users	Much of existing building handed over to other university interests	Re-modelled space for learning interactions with access to some collections; other collections remote
Staff	Allocated across collection services and remote delivery	Substantively professional and online	New skill mixes
Financial resources	Capital focused impact spilling into Faculty space	Almost solely resource and operational	Shared capital with Learning areas; better value from resources and operational

As kindly agreed to by Andrew Wells; written by Steve O'Connor

Case study 3: CAVAL Ltd, Melbourne, Australia

(As written by Steve O'Connor and agreed to by the Caval Board)

Background

CAVAL Ltd is a consortium based in Melbourne, established in 1978. It was established primarily as a cataloguing consortium for the academic libraries in the Australian state of Victoria. In the course of time, the union cataloguing operation grew and was developed by the National Library of Australia into a National Bibliographic utility. The consortium had been established as a company under Australian Company Law. At the time of constructing the new scenario, it operated essentially a small multi-lingual cataloguing operation and an emerging storage facility of low-use research materials for the owners of the company. The company's board of directors were looking for new directions which might make the company more stable and sustainable. They were also interested in reducing the financial costs to their own libraries. The new CEO ran a widely based scenario planning exercise drawing out three possible scenarios. Only the final scenario which was accepted by the board is included here. This scenario also suggested a new trading name for the company. This name *CAVAL Collaborative Solutions* was adopted and used in all promotional materials while the name CAVAL Limited was retained for legal and company purposes.

Scenario

CAVAL Collaborative Solutions is a dynamic, entrepreneurial company which has grown from its solid beginnings as CAVAL. The company has developed to serve a wide customer base – museums, galleries, archives as well as libraries across Australia, New Zealand and the region while still being owned by Victoria's Vice Chancellors and the State Library Board of Victoria. The service quality, cost efficiency and scope of businesses has, in the early years of the twenty-first century, begun to be more attractive to the private sector. The company is well positioned to serve the wider information community including public and special libraries.

The establishment of the new company has enabled its customers to enjoy an increasing range of professional development opportunities and value-added services with the further benefit of these being achieved in an environment of reducing membership fees and charges.

CAVAL Collaborative Solutions has significantly expanded the range of products and services it offers without diminishing its commitment to its core services of a digital and analogue repository and a national borrowing and authentication service. These services have continued to expand over the years and still are a major focus of the organisation.

In the early stages of its growth CAVAL Collaborative Solutions added a range of new services including training and performance consulting services in partnership with other high-quality providers. This was followed by a recruitment and 'locum' service. A full disaster management and recovery service has also received considerable interest from a range of organisations across the region. The broad range of services provided the cash reserves to develop new markets and introduce new technologies.

The success of CAVAL Collaborative Solutions in Victoria quickly attracted the interest of libraries across the nation as well as in New Zealand and the Asia-Pacific region. The involvement of other libraries has added significantly to the critical mass of resources which can now be made available to the staff, students, researchers and wider community who can access the print and electronic resources using the latest technologies and delivery systems. The new services and new technologies mean that the organisation increasingly provides service transparently to library users, often through the traditional market of the libraries themselves. This new focus has created an even stronger culture of customer service within CAVAL Collaborative Solutions.

While CAVAL Collaborative Solutions is increasingly able to distribute services directly to users, the organisation also uses the available technology to enable its members to over-brand services with their own logo and identity. This allows members to significantly expand the range of offerings to their users without adding to their infrastructure and costs. They are able to concentrate their intellectual and financial resources to provide the highest level of direct customer services while allowing CAVAL Collaborative Solutions to provide as a partner the time-consuming and technologically sophisticated infrastructure tasks so necessary for the provision of information services in the new century.

The success of CAVAL Collaborative Solutions in serving the region's libraries has created interest from other cultural institutions which are also seeking efficiencies in a world of tight budgets and increased calls on their resources.

The CARM repository has grown significantly to house several million volumes, in print and electronic form, and is a leading part of a National Repository system occupying several sites across the nation. It is also a high-tech repository for resources from galleries, museums and archives. The focus is on providing access to digital and analogue information irrespective of the location of the client. The company's skill base has enabled effective extension to the provision of a Digital Imaging and Indexing Service which is much in demand.

CAVAL Collaborative Solutions is continuing its strategy of investing in leading edge technologies to manage and make available resources to its clients. The expertise which has been built by CAVAL Collaborative Solutions in deploying new technologies has created a major business opportunity with information management and consultancy forming a high-revenue business unit in its own right.

CAVAL Collaborative Solutions's innovative focus has also led to its recent strategic alliance with an innovative Australian owned multi-media web company. Partnerships and commercially strategic alliances represent major opportunities, and a major direction, for CAVAL Collaborative Solutions and its customers.

The size, reach and innovation of its services also ensure that the organisation is a key, and equal, player alongside the great and small library and cultural networks of the world.

New services, strategic partnerships and new customers are the watchwords of CAVAL Collaborative Solutions.

Case study 4: SOLINET scenarios

(As kindly agreed to by Kate Nevins, Solinet/Lyrasis)

Background

Members were asked to participate in the discussion via an e-mail invitation. Those able to attend received a copy of all three scenarios prior to the meeting date. Scenarios were developed to depict libraries three to five years into the future, without reference to specific library types or sizes.

Discussion groups contained 10 to 20 people. The discussion was formally facilitated to obtain feedback through the following process:

1. Introduction of all participants, purpose of discussion, and context of scenario planning.

2. Full group divided into three small groups, each to discuss a different scenario and answer the following questions:

   (a) What aspects of the scenario are likely for libraries in 3–5 years?

   (b) What aspects of the scenario are not likely in 3–5 years?

   (c) Is there anything important that is missing? (Are there likely changes in 3–5 years that are not represented in the scenario?)

3. Small groups reported out on their discussions.

4. Small groups reconvened and discussed 'What can SOLINET do to help your libraries reach the desired future?'

Notes and flip charts were kept for each discussion, and the results of those were combined into a summary report. A link to the finished, web-based report was emailed to all individuals invited to participate in the discussions.

Scenario A

Moving to the Front of the House

This library is serving its community with energy and drive. Resources (staff, collections, and space) have been re-allocated to directly support service goals. Staff resources in particular focus on 'front-of-shop' operations, to ensure that the library remains as relevant to the information needs of its community as possible. The library is re-evaluating and frequently outsourcing repetitive and routine processes that do not directly serve users. At the same time, collaborations with non-library organisations are increasing, to better meet a range of community needs within the context of the library (for example, academic libraries are collaborating with tutoring, advising, and technology services on campus to support students, and public libraries are collaborating with local government agencies and businesses to expand access to community services).

Collections are a mix of analogue and digital resources. The book is still important to most users, and digitised materials available in paper format through such services as on-demand printing make up an increasingly large part of the library's acquisitions. The library is very conscious of the cost of storage for valuable but lesser-used library collections, and it has sought ways and means to store these materials in off-site facilities. Not only is this more cost effective, but off-site storage also frees up more space for user services.

Cost is a significant driver for the administration of the library and its governing agency. The need to justify plans and account for expenditures is paramount. While the library does prefer to have regular suppliers who understand their information and service need, cost is a primary factor in decision-making. To meet accountability expectations, the library relies on assessments of its performance relative to similar organisations. It also invests more resources into obtaining feedback from users and providing 'return on investment' reports to the community.

- *Services* are designed to meet assessed needs and be accountable to a defined community of users.

- *Technology* is used to support service to users and re-design of traditional library functions to reduce costs.

- *Collections* are developed to meet immediate needs of users, with reliance on interlibrary lending to supplement local resources.

- *Buildings* are community and service-oriented, although funds to renovate are limited.
- *Staffs* are skilled adapters of technology, with expertise in service management, assessment, and contracting.

Scenario B

The Lithe Physical and Digital Library

The library collection in 2010 has actually shrunk in physical size, but it delivers much more digital resource than it was ever able to deliver as a mixed-media library in previous years. The content of the digital media in the library includes a wide range of materials, from print through music, art, datasets, and interactive games. Some of the library digital collection is 'born digital' and some also exists in analogue format. Increasingly, the library acts as the repository and venue for digital resources produced throughout its community. While many library users are never actually seen (they access the library from their home, office, classroom, etc.), ever larger groups of users still come to the physical library for collaborative work and study space, socialising, and community services. There is a 'wallpaper' collection of books, but the vast array of resources in the library are digital.

With limited financial buying power, libraries have elected to adopt a strategy of digital delivery for the content they do not hold directly through subscriptions. This has resulted in the delivery of material in digital form that had been only available in print form previously. Wholesale retro-conversion of print resources into digital is still economically challenging for most libraries, but digital conversion is possible for material of immediate use and high value (such as unique, local, and special collections). Digitisation and technology extend the library's resource reach beyond the region into national and international realms.

The library maintains a strong but flexible staffing arrangement and secures the skill experts it needs when it needs them. It does this so that it can offer the best services to a wide range of users, including an enthusiastic new group of Generation Y and younger users who have different styles of study and service expectations than other groups. With constantly evolving technology and user expectations, libraries invest significant resources in staying ahead of the curve. Although the library still has a strong sense of its physical presence, it is keenly aware that even more usage of its services and content occurs in homes and offices across its community. Users mix the content received from the library with the huge amount of 'free-to-air' resources they can access from the web. They are able to do this with a sharp appreciation of how to evaluate content from both sources because of education programmes the library offers both in person and remotely.

- *Services* are primarily digital, both to local and remote users.

- *Technology* is the basis for provision of library services and access to library information resources and collections.

- *Collections* are primarily electronic. Print and other analogue formats are being converted to digital formats.

- *Buildings* remain the physical anchor of the library. They serve local users as a community centre and function as the physical base for the staff and technology resources that drive service to all users.

- *Staffs* use forward-thinking technology skills to be community leaders in information technology.

Scenario C

The Collaborative, User-Driven Library

Library services are increasingly customised to meet individual characteristics of their users. Users have a stronger role than ever in the provision of library services, and are active participants in library operations, from design and delivery of information services to selection and organisation of collection resources. The library collaborates with users in providing service. It also collaborates actively with other libraries through local, state, and regional networks and affinity groups, to meet the needs of various and different shared constituencies.

User and library collaboration is facilitated by the strong integration of library resources with common web-based search engines, such as Google and Yahoo. Users find library resources through these mechanisms rather than through a stand-alone library catalogue. Through web-based search services, libraries are virtually joined together in a global catalogue of resources.

As a consequence, library technical services have changed. Libraries acquire most new material pre-processed, so they do not need to invest internal staff resources in traditional cataloguing. Cataloguing that does occur at the library uses more basic metadata standards defined by international organisations, with the primary goal of ensuring discoverability of library resources through web search services. Librarians can easily source their in-house cataloguing and interlibrary borrowing programmes by directly searching the records of all libraries through Google or Yahoo. State and regional networks provide coordination among their libraries to facilitate lending programmes. At the same time, 'folksonomies' are increasingly created and managed by libraries and their users, as another means to customise services. This customisation is also evident in collection acquisitions, as more resources are acquired through on-demand publishing and pay-per-view services at the specific request of users.

Library staff are sophisticated technologists, working with others in the community to develop and apply a variety of programs and tools to library services with a focus on those that enhance user collaboration and improve communication and information delivery. Many of these programs are open source. Working collaboratively with other libraries through networks and consortia supports the development of open-source technology in libraries and ensures interoperability.

- *Services* are primarily digital and users are very involved in their design and delivery; the library is a collaborator and facilitator in providing information services.

- *Technology* is developed by the library to facilitate services to users; it is used to streamline internal processes and support collaboration among users and libraries.

- *Collections* are primarily digital, more often leased than purchased, and selection and acquisition decisions are often driven directly by users.

- *Buildings* support the library infrastructure and provide collaborative community workspace.

- *Staffs* apply forward-thinking technology skills to library operations and to building collaboration and community among users.

Case study 5: Public library

(As written by Cal Shepherd. With kind permission of Lyrasis)

Scenarios[3]

Role of the library in the community

The following scenarios encompass two important trends: funding for libraries and the library's place in the market or relevance to today's user. With the assumption that libraries will experience decreased funding across the board, the scenarios project three different outcomes pertaining to the library's relevance in its community: the library will take on increased relevance, the library's relevance will remain stable but services will become increasingly virtual, and the library's relevance will decrease.

Increased relevance

Community and academic coffers have been depleted by crisis responses to a general economic decline along with decreased tax revenue. Funding for libraries is less available. Despite the budget shortfall, however, and perhaps because of it, users continue to use their libraries in record numbers. The cost to individuals of buying books, home computers and e-book readers, along with fees for accessing digital content continues to be a significant barrier for large segments of the population. The importance of digital resources is rising and the library has positioned itself as a source for this e-content. At the same time, government and other services are continuing to move online and the library is increasingly seen as the source for these services.

All libraries are buying fewer print resources and more digital resources every year. The physical facilities are increasingly serving as the gathering place for users –

community centre, group study space and learning centre. The library offers learning programmes that are in high demand by the local community and faculty alike and is widely viewed as a valuable partner in community service and education. The library undertakes regular assessments both to ascertain service area needs and to gather data to demonstrate return on investment (ROI).

Staff resources are focused on direct public service and staff cuts have hit especially hard in the technical services area. As a result the library has had to outsource more and streamline back-end activities while direct service to users is increasing. This reduction in technical services is offset by increased customer-created and customer-donated content.

The library fulfils a service role in its community and is widely seen as a resource for service rather than an information resource.

Stable relevance/increasingly virtual

Libraries continue to support their communities as an information resource. Increasingly patrons are using library resources virtually and are demanding remote access to library resources and services. For many library patrons the browsing experience has become a virtual phenomenon rather than a physical reality. As a consequence, library catalogues and websites are quickly becoming more and more user friendly.

In addition to virtual browsing, the library's collection is increasingly virtual. With the exception of magazines and newspapers, every single piece of print material is an item that is either requested online for pickup at the library location, a print on demand copy, or an item borrowed (ILL) from another library. With fewer physical holdings, the increasingly virtual collection frees up space in the library building; indeed the largest growth area in library services is the extension of virtual activities. The library has an active presence in Second Life and offers frequent webinars and online classes. Its online book group is very popular, as are the other virtual clubs that the library sponsors. Those patrons who do come through the library doors are doing so to self-serve or to take advantage of the quiet study and other space provided.

The skill set needed by library staff is changing rapidly although there is no funding for staff development or retooling of staff skills. With the emphasis on virtual services, the library is depending more on volunteers to supplement the limited staff who don't have the requisite technical expertise. An enthusiastic group of Generation Y and younger users is helping the library in its move into the virtual arena by contributing to tagging and other Web 2.0 efforts. At the same time their different styles of study and service expectations are putting a strain on the library's ability to deliver expected services.

The library serves as an information resource for its community of users, who want and expect to find the right information with or without the service provided by the library staff.

Decreased relevance

The amount of time spent reading by the American people continues to decline year after year. Costs of new Internet, mobile phone, audio, and visual devices have plummeted and digital content is accessible by just about everyone from anywhere any time. Advances in technology are making interactive education experiences available in dorms or even at home as much as in the classroom. Because of declining door counts, circulation, and other service measures, the library is seen as being increasingly irrelevant with the exception of its electronic resources. County and university officials are allocating resources to meet more pressing needs and, as a result, the library's funding is steadily declining. Print collections are stagnant, staff has been reduced, and new library buildings are not being erected. While the library is esteemed in its community it is struggling to stay afloat using interlibrary loan to make up for ever larger gaps in the collection.

The expectations of library users for library services are in a downward spiral as the library increasingly is unable to meet their needs. The library is viewed as a repository for books whether anyone uses those books or not. The library has an active friends group along with a committed cadre of volunteers made up mostly of retirees. These loyal supporters love books and want to do everything possible to make sure the library's collection is well preserved. The library building with its imposing architecture is often used as the host site for large events such as swearing in the mayor or the installation of a new provost.

Library staff continue to catalogue materials and offer programmes but increasingly users are accessing e-resources remotely without entering the building. Because of the declining customer base the library café closed its doors last year. The library offers public access PCs and group study space which are appreciated by users but not heavily used.

The library is viewed as valuable historical resource (much like a museum) and user expectations for library services are uniformly low.

Case study 6: The possible world of library consortia

(As written by Solinet/Lyrasis staff.
With kind permission of Lyrasis)

These scenarios were drawn up by staff at SOLINET. They are provided here with the kind permission of SOLINET.

Scenario A

The United States of Consortia

Growth in centralised funding for provision of electronic resources and library technology/support services through statewide networks/consortia has increased the power of these organisations in provision of services to both publicly and privately-funded libraries (the latter buying into the network as a more cost-effective means of acquiring resources/services than negotiating directly). Libraries find it easier to go to the statewide consortia than to deal with multiple consortia for different services or to figure out which consortia can provide the best deal on competing services.

As a result, consortia are all state-based and provide services only within their state. Sub-state or local consortia have been consolidated and either gone out of business or operate under the governance of the state consortia (as local 'field' offices). Regional consortia are gone, and the state consortia form partnerships with each other as needed on a national level. There is little if any competition between state consortia.

Members or participants within the state consortia cooperate on the pursuit and administration of funding (from the state legislature and other sources, such as LSTA), in support of a statewide agenda of services. Decision-making is centralised, and the consortia often (but not always) exist within a state government agency. Membership is automatic for all libraries in the state. Programmes are defined based on the needs of the libraries within the state, and so vary from state to state; programmes can include licensing, resource-sharing systems, courier and delivery services, shared technology systems (ILS, OPAC, etc.), digitisation, and continuing education. State consortia serve public, K-12, and academic libraries, in some cases with shared and in others with distinct programmes.

- *Infrastructure*: formal organisations, often governed by state agencies

- Geographic service area: state level

- *Membership*: all libraries within the state (there is no decision to become or not become a member; it is automatic)

- *Funding model*: state appropriation and federal fund (LSTA) administration

- *Programmes*: statewide resource-sharing, licensing, continuing education, courier/delivery services, and technology implementation/support (shared systems?)

Scenario B

Consortia rationalised

Competing interests among a large number of library consortia and stalled or constricted funding have led libraries to limit their engagement in consortia. While still committed to the value of cooperation, libraries are choosing to be members of only those one or two consortia that provide the most direct benefit. At the same time, consolidation of some activities at the state level, such as basic e-resource acquisition through statewide networks, means that some services libraries used to acquire through independent consortia are now provided through state agencies. As a result, libraries affiliate with consortia in two ways: one is an automatic affiliation through a state group (e.g. state consortia, statewide network, or state agency), the other is an individual affiliation with like organisations for a shared programme/service that is not provided through the state.

State-based consortia/networks provide specific programmes as mandated and funded by the state. They vary from state to state, but tend to be limited in scope to those activities that are common to libraries throughout the state, are logically handled on a statewide level, and/or are funded by a significant level of state resource (such as e-resource acquisitions or courier services). Affiliation is automatic for libraries within the state, although each state's engagement of multiple types of libraries varies (academic, public, K-12, private vs. publicly funded, etc.). Services provided through the state organisations are funded by state appropriations.

Programme-based consortia are independent organisations without geographic boundaries. They exist to meet common needs of members, in particular those that are not being met through the locally defined state organisations. Membership is a decision made by an individual library based on their organisation's need for specific programmes or services (such as shared ILS, digitisation, unique e-resource acquisition, shared collections, etc.). Programmatic consortia have clear and focused missions, services, and benefits for members. They are funded by dues, fees, member-contributed resources, and/or grants. Members drive the agenda of the consortia. Competition among independent consortia for members, and libraries' inability to belong to multiple consortia, has resulted in a few, strong consortia with limited overlap in focus.

- Infrastructure: formal organisations
- Geographic service area: some state-based, others programme-based so no geographic focus

- Membership: automatic for state-based; individual library decision for programme-based

- Funding model: state appropriation/LSTA for state-based; a mix of dues and fees for programme-based

- Programmes: state-based consortia focus on those activities funded for all libraries with state appropriations, such as licenses to shared e-resources; programme-based consortia focus on cooperation in a range of areas depending on shared interests of their members, such as digitisation or shared ILS systems.

Scenario C

The Wild World of Consortia (Networked Consortia, or Consortia 2.0)

Consortia proliferate in the Web 2.0 world, where social networking enables the development of relationships among libraries at a grassroots level. Individual staff network with like-minded peers at organisations around the world, forming both formal and informal consortia to address common issues or needs. The consortia environment is extremely fluid, with groups evolving and dissolving as interest waxes and wanes. Most informal consortia mutate rapidly as trends change or directions shift with development of new technologies.

Most consortia are informal. A library's participation in informal consortia is driven by the interests of individual employees; if the employee leaves, the library's participation in the consortia is likely to end, too. Informal consortia tend to operate on a volunteer basis. Funding for resources the consortia may want to acquire on behalf of the participants is contributed directly by the participating libraries (for example, a group purchase of a specific e-resource).

Fewer formal consortia exist. Those that do are independent organisations with a great deal of flexibility and adaptability, aggressively engaged in innovation on behalf of library members. Affiliation is at the library level, and funding is dependent on dues, fees, contributions, and/or grants. Members must see direct value in return for participation, and consortia spend resources on member recruitment as well as retention. Competition among formal consortia can be intense in areas of programme overlap. In addition to providing programmes/products directly to members, formal consortia are valued in part for their infrastructure: the predictable availability of expertise and resources. They may also provide infrastructure support for some informal consortia.

- Infrastructure: many informal and a few formal organisations
- Geographic service area: generally none
- Membership: individual by institution or employee
- Funding model: wide variety; many informal are completely supported by volunteers
- Programmes: wide array, from product and service provision to information exchange

Notes

1. O'Connor, S. (2009). 'Steering a future through scenarios: Into the academic library of the future'. *Journal of Academic Librarianship* 35(1): 60.
2. Ibid., p. 59.
3. Permission has been granted by Lyrasis to use these scenarios.

10

Implementation and the impact of change

Peter Sidorko

This chapter

This book has illustrated the manner in which scenario planning can be adopted. We can use it as a decision-making tool, as a strategic planning tool or as a tool for initiating and preparing an organisation for change. While the first two of these include aspects of change, it is primarily the last that this chapter will address. This chapter will highlight some of the issues surrounding organisational change and while recognising that scenario planning encompasses many of these issues, there are still matters that need further attention.

Change, demolition and reconstruction

We live in turbulent times. If I had been sleeping for the past 15 years and awoke to find the world that we inhabit today, I would be astounded by what had occurred during a relatively short period. If I had slept for 25 years I would be simply dumbfounded. The same might be argued for any period of time, yet the degree to which the information world has changed in recent times has been exceptionally transformational. I recently received an e-mail newsletter from my bank urging me to 'Look beyond the uncertainties' when it comes to investments. Of course they are referring to the uncertainties that the financial crisis of recent times has brought. They are, in their attention-grabbing way, advising me to undertake some scenario planning. As has been mentioned throughout this book, we undergo planning in our personal lives every day. Encapsulated in this planning is the creation of scenarios which lead us to make certain choices, even though, in some cases, we will not be fully cognizant of the repercussions of making these choices. While a large part of scenario planning is about 'looking beyond the uncertainties', imagining a future as it were, these uncertainties cannot be fully neglected as they will be deeply influential in the entire process. And realistically, how often are we even capable of looking beyond uncertainties?

Two of the significant themes recurring within these pages have been the inevitability of change and the ability for all of us to make choices and therefore, insofar as possible, take charge of these and influence changes. Recent global catastrophic events have perhaps challenged that view. To what extent could the devastating effects of the 2004 tsunami or the earthquakes in Haiti and Chile in 2010 have been minimised? Given the extent of these catastrophes, the answer is obviously very small. But even preparing for minor disasters, which most libraries do in the form of disaster preparedness planning, represents some form of scenario planning. Choices are made during such a planning exercise: what type of disasters will we plan for; what degree of damage is to be catered for; how much in the way of resources do we assign? At the annual University of Hong Kong Leadership Institute,[1] change is always a dominating theme. Throughout the four-day residential Institute, participants are assigned a case study, which enables them to work in a small, hopefully cohesive, group and to further explore the themes raised in the formal Institute programme. In recent years the case study has centered on the total destruction of a (fictitious) academic library. Participants are essentially asked to rebuild that library, although not explicitly stated as a physical entity, by responding to a series of questions that challenge their current thoughts on what constitutes an academic library and what the future might hold. Of course, it is relatively simple to devise a plan that simply reconstructs what exists today, and for some participants this is the manner in which they respond. But is planning an academic library today, based on today's needs, an effective solution? The three or four or even more years that it will take to build the library will render the constructed edifice obsolete. Like these workshop participants, many of us would opt for a scenario that is readily identifiable to us but which may not be the best outcome. Even in an artificial environment such as a workshop, many of us are still reluctant to grasp radical changes that question not only the way we conduct our business but the very business in which we operate.

Why are many people so fundamentally averse, or at least reluctant, to envisioning an alternative future? Is this really something that we should do? Or is it the job of library leaders, and library leaders alone? There are no short answers to these questions, and it must be recognised that introducing scenario planning as a change process may not necessarily guarantee successful change. There are further considerations.

The human side of change

In any organisational change process, the first and foremost consideration for any leader is that of the human condition within the organisation. There are two aspects to this: first, the individual human condition and individual responses to change; and second, the organisational culture. Changing an organisation's culture is impossible without first defining what the culture is, what aspects you wish to change, understanding how this culture has evolved and how it might be changed. Many definitions abound as to what organisational culture is or is not, and many of these have a reasonable degree of similarity. Edgar Schein provides many useful perspectives in attempting to define culture (Schein, 1985). One most relevant to this discussion, and which will again prove useful when assessing the degree of success of the changes, is that it is the

> deeper level of *basic assumptions* and *beliefs* that are shared by members of an organisation, that operate unconsciously, and that define in a basic 'taken-for-granted' fashion an organisation's view of itself and its environment (ibid., p. 6).

Let us first address the latter element of the human component in change, the organisational culture. Most scenario planning exercises will be undertaken in groups. The examples used throughout this book have all emphasised group interactivity as a key element to the processes. This is a key element to implementing a scenario planning exercise as the degree of participation will influence the extent of acceptance with the follow-up implementation and the ensuing changes that will be required. As a group participative process, the impact of organisational culture will be inevitable. If we step back to Schein's definition, which essentially states that it is the set of shared influences that dictates how the organisation views itself and its environment and therefore how it behaves, we can immediately appreciate that any manager using scenario planning should be well aware of these influences.

Just like any other organisation, libraries too perpetuate their own organisational culture. While there may be a degree of similarity in organisational culture across libraries, and more specifically across libraries from the same sector, it would be foolish to assume that these similarities are deep or deeply rooted. Similarities across libraries' organisational cultures occur because all librarians are trained in library and information science. Most librarians are also members of professional library bodies and associations. Many of these associations provide standards for librarians to adopt, including aspects of quality service, equity of access and ethical practices. Additionally, librarians share a unique nomenclature and jargon. It can be readily discerned how such commonalities may affect organisational culture to some degree. However, other factors that contribute to organisational culture should immediately dispel any notion that all libraries enjoy the same organisational culture. The basic assumptions and beliefs that form the culture are accrued and refined over a sometimes very long period of time. These basic building blocks may have been initiated at the highest level of the organisation but would have evolved quite significantly. Similarly, most organisations have people in power, i.e. management, as well as people with 'informal' power. In other words there are those who are not necessarily in management positions but who hold a strong influence over activities of the organisation as well as the behaviour of staff. That is not to say that the influences of organisational culture and the informal power brokers should be eradicated, even if that were naively considered remotely possible, but that there needs to be awareness of them and they should be harnessed for their ability, if at all possible, to enhance the process or to at least minimise their likely negative impact. Given this, it is obviously necessary that a leader in an organisation is cognizant of the culture that exists within the organisation and that a new recruit to the position, for example, would do well to develop this familiarity before embarking on a lengthy change process, be it initiated through scenario planning or some other mechanism.

At an individual level, the response to change is a highly personal experience. While an experienced leader well attuned to staff idiosyncrasies may feel confident in predicting how an individual may react to a change process, the reality is that previous responses to change may have little bearing on how that individual reacts in the future. So while responses to change are unique to individuals they will not be consistent with every individual over time. Chapter 5 presented a classic organisational change progression that most organisations will experience. To recap, these four stages consisted of complacency, denial, chaos, then transformation. These four stages are recognizable to most managers and leaders as periods that the *organisation* endures (or enjoys, depending on one's perspective) during periods of change. At a more personal and individual level, these stages can be reinterpreted into more human responses to change, which will obviously then inform the organisational stages. Many authors (e.g. Elrod and Tippett, 2002; Zell, 2003) have likened individual and organisational responses to change with those identified by Elisabeth Kübler-Ross in her famous work, *On Death and Dying* (1969). Obviously organisational change cannot be likened to death, yet the five stages identified by Kübler-Ross will be readily identifiable with any experienced manager who has encountered difficulties implementing change. These five stages are: denial, anger, bargaining, depression and, finally, acceptance. It is interesting to note that while Kübler-Ross documented these five stages in her landmark 1969 work, Mwalimu Imara (1975: 163) recognised the same change process in the sixth chapter of the book of Isaiah in the Old Testament, where the prophet Isaiah experiences these same five stages as he faces his task. While the difficulty in the change process can be documented dating back to 700 BC, some 2,700 years before Kübler-Ross, it provides little solace for today's manager in knowing that human reactions to change date back as far as they appear to.

By placing these five expected stages within the context of a scenario planning exercise, it is conceivable that several of them could be potentially disruptive to the process. Beginning with denial, it is instantly recognisable by managers that a certain number of staff will fail to appreciate the necessity for change and therefore see no value whatsoever in undertaking a scenario planning exercise. One of the critical phases of introducing change, be it through a scenario planning exercise or otherwise, is to create an environment where it can be recognised by all in the organisation (an overly ambitious task, perhaps) that change simply must occur. The livelihood of the organisation, the continuity of employment or other risks must be stressed as a means of garnering support for the exercise. Kotter (1996) is a particularly strong advocate of this. While change models should be adopted and followed with a degree of caution, there is much merit in Kotter's work, particularly his first three preparation phases, a critical stage that many change initiators fail to fully exploit. The first step of the preparation phase of Kotter's model is to *establish a sense of urgency*. The sense of urgency is created from the factor or factors that are necessitating the change. These could have arisen from internal or external pressures or problems that have been identified with the existing organisation. It is the responsibility of organisational leaders to ensure that these pressures or problems are well communicated to members of the organisation. As such, the urgency is communicated and established. Sheltering staff from such pressures will only lead to rejection, or at best suspicion of related change processes, including the initial and subsequent stages of scenario planning.

While I have indicated that the pace of change in the information and library sector has been transformational in recent years, this is really only the case relative to the earlier history of the information professions. This is certainly the case when we compare ourselves with other professions where changes have had immediate and devastating impacts. Consider, for example, the business and finance sectors, where currency fluctuations and share market prices can have an instantly dramatic impact resulting in corporate closure and extinction. It is very rare that libraries face such immediate threats. As such it can be difficult to develop this need for urgency with people who can see change but who also realise that tomorrow will be another day and the library will continue. In other words, due to our previous, relatively stable and continuous existence a certain degree of complacency that may have crept in could lead to difficulty in establishing the sense of urgency, so this part of the process is extremely important in libraries. It is also a part of the change process that scenario planning manages very effectively.

In order to establish the need for change as a precursor to any planning, the message must be delivered and must be delivered using language that is understandable by all involved in the process. Understandable language is language that is appropriate to the *people* receiving the message and to the *content* of the message that is being transmitted. For example, in a large organisation it may be necessary to relay the same message using different approaches and different vocabularies. Think of large academic libraries, for example, and the diversity of staff that work in them, with skill sets and educational backgrounds as varied as the number of people employed. In other words, one message may need to be relayed in multiple ways. The need for communication does not end once the urgency for change has been established. Many authors note that change processes fail due to a paucity of ongoing communication, communication that is disingenuous and the lack of meaningful two-way communication. This also rings true during a scenario planning stage of change. There are, however, some notable peculiarities regarding communication and in particular the style of language that should be used in scenario planning. While much scenario planning is undertaken in the corporate world, the language of the corporate world is incongruous to what is trying to be realised through the scenario planning exercises. The corporate world's language is littered with formality and jargon, abbreviations and acronyms, and is normally complicated, proper and rigid. None of these are characteristics that would strongly help us to engender our 'perceptions about alternative future environments in which [our] decisions might be played out' (Schwartz, 1996, p.4) or facilitate our ability to 'dream about our own future' (ibid.) and create alternative views of the future that enable us to be receptive and amenable to not only the probable but the possible. The language that is needed is the language of myths and stories, of visions and extremes, of fluidity and openness.

The significance of communication that is appropriate, consistent and continuous cannot be underestimated during any change process, and this is especially true of a change process utilising scenario planning. As scenario planning encompasses the envisioning of futures and usually includes a wide range of participation from staff with varying communication skills, these envisioned futures need to be communicated effectively so that a consistent understanding of them is possible. This requires sound communication skills from not only the leaders and facilitators of the process but all participants. While noting that communication skills vary significantly among workers, including library employees, patience and practical listening skills are also required.

Getting involved and involvement

Chapter 5 of this book set out the need to incorporate the involvement and views of 'as many people as possible' when it comes to developing possible future directions of the organisation. The degree of employee participation in any library's scenario planning process will depend on the purpose which the process is striving towards, the type of organisation and its leadership. In current management philosophy, the benefits behind a participative management approach also apply to scenario planning. Perhaps first among these is that choices made (decisions) through a participative process are more likely to enjoy greater ownership and acceptance which can lead to increased productivity, quality and employee satisfaction. Additionally, greater participation should lead to a wider range of ideas and solutions as more brainpower is available. In a scenario planning context this is especially important as the need to envision futures will derive more possibilities with greater participation. At this point it is worth returning to Howard Gardner's *The Theory of Multiple Intelligences*, as discussed in Chapter 5, in order to highlight the further potential advantages of greater participation. When brought to the scenario planning process, Gardner's seven intelligences (Intrapersonal, Interpersonal, Bodily/Kinesthetic, Musical, Spatial, Logical/Mathematical and Linguistic) could well serve to enrich the process by providing a wider array of future possibilities as exemplified through these intelligences. There are also potential benefits, as noted previously, through greater employee acceptance of scenarios and the preferred scenario, as well as any consequent changes, when employees feel they have participated in the process that arrived at these. There are also longer term benefits for employees resulting from their participation in the scenario planning exercises. For example, Chermack and Nimon (2008) also found that those who participated in scenario planning exercises subsequently demonstrated a more intuitive-based decision-making style than those who did not.

Finally, with the appropriate environment and scene setting by a facilitator, encouraging active participation in scenario planning processes can often be a rewarding experience as participants may tend to open up and be more responsive in terms of using their imagination as they may deem the process less threatening than working on some more immediate change-related activities. Chapter 6 provided a strategic breakdown of how a preferred scenario can be devised. These seven steps form a logical and systematic process that most should find unintimidating. The exception, as noted in Chapter 6, may be that some library staff feel affronted through the imagining of possibilities that serve to dismantle the very environment to which they had grown comfortably accustomed. To some extent this affront is allayed by the fact that the process is future-focused and driven, and these staff may well soon recognise that there is a certain safety in this distance in time. This of course is a positive thing and will help the seven-step process to arrive at a participative and future-focused preferred scenario. The downside of this is that when it does come time to implement the changes to help arrive at the preferred scenario, certain staff may – indeed some most likely will – feel somewhat cheated by the process. The future, after all, is intended to happen.

Following through and embedding the change

The process of getting people involved in developing the preferred scenario that actually does result in a satisfactory outcome and a sense of ownership by participants is not the end of the journey. While this part of the journey will undoubtedly serve to facilitate many of the resultant changes, there will still be those unwilling, or at least concerned, to bring these changes to fruition. These will include staff who did not participate in the process, but as I have noted above, it will also include staff who had participated, imagined the future and seen it as a distant possibility, but who now face the reality and implications of that process.

A plethora of literature exists on managing and leading change in organisations; one of the very best, Kotter (1996), has been referred to already. In the library and information service environment, there is also a significant body of literature related to successful change. Ian Smith (2006, 2008) echoes many of Kotter's strategies and sentiments, yet provides a uniquely library-centric approach to these. Many change strategists advocate a multi-step approach to implementing change. These steps are broadly arranged under three phases in the process, namely preparation, action and grounding. Some authors of change literature, Kotter and Smith included, argue that too much attention is focused on the middle stage, leaving the preparation and grounding phases as afterthoughts.

In a scenario planning situation it can be generally accepted that, if the process has been managed effectively, then the preparatory phase should be well covered as by its very nature this is part of what scenario planning is intended to achieve. The 'action' phase is when the changes are implemented and, as many managers are keen to see these happen, it is the phase where most attention is aimed. Outlined above are some of the strategies employed that can assist with the organisational change process. Once again, many of these are also already embedded in the scenario planning process but will require additional energy and resources beyond that process in order to effect the change. Most notable among these are: (i) providing extensive communication that is appropriate, targeted and consistent; as well as (ii) ensuring that participation is also as extensive as possible. Participation at this stage, however, is quite different to the scenario planning phase where the futures were imagined. During this phase the future is realised! Participation, therefore, comes in the form of decision-making on how best to effect the necessary changes, how to decide on the particular timeframe for each of these changes, the identification of different roles for individuals and so on. This will serve to further engender a sense of ownership achieved during the process of creating the preferred scenario.

The final phase of the change process, or cycle as many authors choose to define it, is the grounding or embedding phase. Like the preparation phase, this final phase is often ignored by managers or at least under-represented in the overall change process. The reasons for this can be instantly recognisable to any manager. Change takes time and during the initial phases, or the action phase alone if that has been the approach, a degree of tiredness, perhaps even boredom, may creep into the manager's psyche. When the change has been made a sense of achievement is realised. A long, sometimes hard-fought, battle has ended. Things are now different and as they were seemingly intended. It must be recognised that the stage that appears to be the end of the change process, when 'the most visible parts of a change program have been completed' (Smith, 2008: p. 27), then the 'process of change does not stop' (ibid.). As Smith notes, the reason that this is necessary is that a certain 'organisational inertia' may soon creep into the process or a desire by some key players in the process to return to the old ways of doing things. It must be kept in mind that these attitudes are made possible as a result of the release of focus from the manager/management who chooses to relish what appears to be successful change and therefore is self-rewarded by keeping a distance from the end result. This loss of focus can – although not always, as the significance of the change will be one factor here – lead to a rapid dismantling of all the good that had been achieved.

In order to overcome the effects of stopping too early there are two possible approaches. The first of these is to persevere, maintain focus and keep a watchful eye over the changes. The reality of this, however, is that library managers are busy people and this may not fit within already tight schedules. Additionally, how does one know when the watchful eye can be relaxed? The second of these is to undertake an 'honest evaluation' (Smith, 2008). As Smith notes, some difficult questions must be asked, including: 'Have the expected benefits been achieved?'; 'What can be learned from how the change was handled?'; 'What might have been done better?'; and 'What remains to be done?' (Smith, 2008, p. 27). The emphasis here must be on providing an 'honest' assessment. While it may be rewarding for a manager to enjoy what appears to be a successful change, a failure to fully embed that change through careful observation and evaluation may lead to a dismantling that would have wasted a large amount of time, energy and resources of, not only the manager, but all the staff involved in the process. Finally, for those staff in the process who were inspired by the changes and keen for them to occur, significant resentment will encroach, as will a loss of respect for the manager who was unable to fully see the change through to successful completion.

Change and scenario planning

While it has been said in this book and elsewhere that change is a given, there is general consensus that the change that is taking place is quite irregular, or discontinuous. In other words, there are incidents when the change is quite dramatic (disruptive change) and there are other times when the change is almost trivial or incremental. The difficulty this presents for organisations, and especially managers, is that it is a struggle to anticipate the degree of impending change as we cannot rely on the past as our guide, given the irregularity and discontinuity of previous change. This book has in many ways provided a blueprint for change, quite irrespective of whether the change is likely to be trivial or transformational. Embarking on a scenario planning process represents one of the more forward-looking, yet energy and resource consuming, change tools that a library or other organisation can adopt. As such, investing in scenario planning as a change process cannot be done in isolation from other change practices and principles. The investment is far too great for it to be done in isolation. Yet the rewards that await the leaders of change who adopt these practices in unison are far too great to be neglected.

Note

1. The University of Hong Kong Libraries (2010). *HKU Libraries Leadership Institute*. Accessible at: *http://lib.hku.hk/leadership* (accessed 18 March 2010).

Further reading

Arnoldi, J. (2009). *Risk: An introduction*. Cambridge: Polity Press.

Auletta, K. (2009). *Googled: The end of the world as we know it*. New York: Penguin Press.

Benkler, Y. (2006). *The Wealth of Networks: How social production transforms markets and freedom*. New Haven: Yale University Press.

Bilton, C. (2007). *Management and Creativity: From creative industries to creative management*. Malden, MA: Blackwell Publishing.

Brafman, O. and Brafman, R. (2008). *Sway: The irresistible pull of irrational behavior* (1st edn). New York: Doubleday.

Brown, J. S. and Duguid, P. (2000). *The Social Life of Information*. Boston: Harvard Business School Press.

Chermack, T. J. and Nimon, K. (2008). 'The effects of scenario planning on participant decision-making style', *Human Resource Development Quarterly* 19(4): 351–72.

Chew, C. (2009). *Strategic Positioning in Voluntary and Charitable Organizations*. New York: Routledge.

Christensen, C. M. (2003; 2000). *The Innovator's Dilemma: The revolutionary book that will change the way you do business* (1 HarperBusiness Essentials edn). New York, N.Y.: HarperBusiness Essentials.

Christensen, C. M., Anthony, S. D. and Roth, E. A. (2004). *Seeing What's Next? Using the theories of innovation to predict industry change*. Boston: Harvard Business School Press.

Elrod, P. and Tippett, D. (2002). 'The "death valley" of change', *Journal of Organizational Change Mangement*, 15(3): 273–91.

Farson, R. E. (1996). *Management of the Absurd: Paradoxes in leadership*. New York: Simon & Schuster.

Fukuyama, F. (2007). *Blindside: How to anticipate forcing events and wild cards in global politics*. Washington, DC: Brookings Institution Press.

Galliers, R., Galliers, R. and Leidner, D. E. (2009). *Strategic Information Management: Challenges and strategies in managing information systems* (4th edn). New York: Routledge.

Goldstone, J. A. (2003). *States, Parties, and Social Movements*. Cambridge, UK and New York: Cambridge University Press.

Hamel, G. and Prahalad, C. K. (1994). *Competing for the Future*. Boston, MA: Harvard Business School Press.

Hawkins, D. E. and Rajagopal, S. (2005). *Sun Tzu and the Project Battleground: Creating project strategy from 'The art of war'*. Basingstoke and New York: Palgrave Macmillan.

Haycock, K. and Sheldon, B. E. (2008). *The Portable MLIS: Insights from the experts*. Westport, CT: Libraries Unlimited.

Imara, M. (1975). 'Dying as the last stage', in E. Kübler-Ross (ed.), *Death: The final stage of growth*. Englewood Cliffs, NJ: Prentice-Hall, 147–63.

Jacobs, D. (2010). *Mapping Strategic Diversity: Strategic thinking from a variety of perspectives*. London and New York: Routledge.

Kotter, J. P. (1996). *Leading Change*. Boston: Harvard Business School Press.

Kressel, H. and Lento, T. V. (2007). *Competing for the Future: How digital innovations are changing the world*. Cambridge: Cambridge University Press.

Kübler-Ross, E. (1969). *On Death and Dying*. New York: Macmillan.

Malone, T. W. (2004). *The Future of Work: How the new order of business will shape your organization, your management style, and your life*. Boston, MA: Harvard Business School Press.

Mant, A. (1999). *Intelligent Leadership* (2nd edn). Crows Nest, NSW: Allen & Unwin.

Marcus, A. A. (2009). *Strategic Foresight: A new look at scenarios* (1st edn). New York: Palgrave Macmillan.

Meyrowitz, J. (1985). *No Sense of Place: The impact of electronic media on social behavior*. New York: Oxford University Press.

Mitroff, I. I. (2004). *Crisis Leadership: Planning for the unthinkable*. Hoboken, NJ: Wiley.

Mlodinow, L. (2008). *The Drunkard's Walk: How randomness rules our lives* (1st edn). New York: Pantheon Books.

Palfrey, J. and Gasser, U. (2008). *Born Digital: Understanding the first generation of digital natives*. New York: Basic Books.

Ralston, B. and Wilson, I. (2006). *The Scenario-Planning Handbook: A practitioner's guide to developing and using scenarios to direct strategy in today's uncertain times*. Mason, OH: Thomson South-Western.

Ringland, G. (2006). *Scenario Planning: Managing for the future* (2nd edn). Chichester, UK and Hoboken, NJ: Wiley.

Schein, E. (1985). *Organisational Culture and Leadership*. San Franciso, CA: Jossey-Bass Publishers.

Schwartz, P. (1996). *The Art of the Long View: Paths to strategic insight for yourself and your company*. New York: Currency Doubleday.

Shirky, C. (2008). *Here Comes Everybody: The power of organizing without organizations*. New York: Penguin Press.

Smith, I. (2006). 'Achieving successful organisational change – do's and don'ts of change management', *Library Management*, 27(4/5), 300–306.

Smith, I. (2008). 'People management – be bold!' *Library Management* 29(1/2): 18–28.

Stead, J. G. and Stead, W. E. (2009). *Management for a Small Planet* (3rd edn). Armonk, NY: M.E. Sharpe.

Stein, H. F. (2007). *Insight and Imagination: A study in knowing and not knowing in organizational life*. Lanham, MD: University Press of America, Inc.

Sunstein, C. R. (2005). *Laws of Fear: Beyond the precautionary principle*. Cambridge;, UK and New York: Cambridge University Press.

Sunstein, C. R. (2006). *Infotopia: How Many Minds Produce Knowledge*. New York: Oxford University Press.

Sunstein, C. R. (2007a). *Worst-Case Scenarios*. Cambridge, MA: Harvard University Press.

Sunstein, C. R. (2007b). *Republic.com 2.0*. Princeton, NJ: Princeton University Press.

Tapscott, D. and Williams, A. D. (2006). *Wikinomics: How mass collaboration changes everything*. New York: Portfolio.

Thaler, R. H. and Sunstein, C. R. (2008). *Nudge: Improving decisions about health, wealth, and happiness*. New Haven, CT: Yale University Press.

Wallace, J. and Erickson, J. (1992). *Hard Drive: Bill Gates and the making of the Microsoft empire*. New York: Wiley.

Watson, R. (2008). *Future Files: 5 trends that will shape the next 50 years*. London: Nicholas Brealey Publisher.

Wright, A. (2007). *Glut: Mastering information through the ages*. Washington, DC: Joseph Henry Press.

Zell, D. (2003), 'Organizational change as a process of

death, dying and rebirth', *Journal of Applied Behavioural Science* 39(1): 73–96.

Zittrain, J. (2008). *The Future of the Internet and How to Stop It*. New Haven, CT: Yale University Press.

Index